THE ELEMENTARY TEACHER'S GUIDE TO THE BEST INTERNET RESOURCES

Content, Lesson Plans, Activities, and Materials

Bárbara C. Cruz
University of South Florida

James A. Duplass
University of South Florida

PEARSON

Merrill
Prentice Hall

Upper Saddle River, New Jersey
Columbus, Ohio

Library of Congress Cataloging-in-Publication Data
Cruz, Bárbara.
The elementary teacher's guide to the best Internet resources: content, lesson plans,
activities, and materials / Bárbara C. Cruz, James A. Duplass.
p. cm.
ISBN 0-13-219270-5 (paperback)
1. Computer network resources—Study and teaching (Elementary)—United States.
2. Internet in education—United States. 3. Curriculum planning—United States.
I. Duplass, James A. II Title.
LB1044.87.C78 2007
372.133′4678—dc22   2005056625

Vice President and Executive Publisher: Jeffery W. Johnston
Executive Editor: Debra A. Stollenwerk
Senior Editorial Assistant: Mary Morrill
Assistant Development Editor: Elisa Rogers
Production Editor: Kris Roach
Production Coordination: GGS Book Services
Design Coordinator: Diane C. Lorenzo
Cover Designer: Terry Rohrback
Cover Image: Index Stock
Production Manager: Susan Hannahs
Director of Marketing: David Gesell
Senior Marketing Manager: Darcy Betts Prybella
Marketing Coordinator: Brian Mounts

This book was set in Minion by GGS Book Services. It was printed and bound by
Courier Corp. The cover was printed by Courier Corp.

Pearson Education Ltd.   Pearson Education Australia Pty. Limited
Pearson Education Singapore Pte. Ltd.   Pearson Education North Asia Ltd.
Pearson Education Canada, Ltd.   Pearson Educación de Mexico, S.A. de C.V.
Pearson Education—Japan   Pearson Education Malaysia Pte. Ltd.

10 9 8 7 6 5 4 3 2 1
ISBN: 0-13-219270-5

To Our Spouses
Anne Duplass
Kevin A. Yelvington

Teacher Preparation Classroom

TEACHER PREP

MERRILL
PRENTICE HALL

Your Class. Their Careers. Our Future. Will your students be prepared?

We invite you to explore our new, innovative and engaging website and all that it has to offer you, your course, and tomorrow's educators! Organized around the major courses pre-service teachers take, the Teacher Preparation site provides media, student/teacher artifacts, strategies, research articles, and other resources to equip your students with the quality tools needed to excel in their courses and prepare them for their first classroom.

This ultimate on-line education resource is available at no cost, when packaged with a Merrill text, and will provide you and your students access to:

Online Video Library. More than 150 video clips—each tied to a course topic and framed by learning goals and Praxis-type questions—capture real teachers and students working in real classrooms, as well as in-depth interviews with both students and educators.

Student and Teacher Artifacts. More than 200 student and teacher classroom artifacts—each tied to a course topic and framed by learning goals and application questions—provide a wealth of materials and experiences to help make your study to become a professional teacher more concrete and hands-on.

Research Articles. Over 500 articles form ASCD's renowned journal *Educational Leadership*. The site also includes Research Navigator, a searchable database of additional educational journals.

Teaching Strategies. Over 500 strategies and lesson plans for you to use when you become a practicing professional.

Licensure and Career Tools. Resources devoted to helping you pass your licensure exam; learn standards, law, and public policies; plan a teaching portfolio; and succeed in your first year of teaching.

How to ORDER *Teacher Prep* for you and your students:

For students to receive a *Teacher Prep* Access Code with this text, instructors **must** provide a special value pack ISBN number on their textbook order form. To receive this special ISBN, please email **Merrill.marketing@ pearsoned.com** and provide the following information:
- Name and Affiliation
- Author/Title/Edition of Merrill text

Upon ordering *Teacher Prep* for their students, instructors will be given a lifetime *Teacher Prep* Access Code.

Preface

DEAR COLLEAGUES:

The promise of the Internet has arrived! Anyone interested in improving the education of children should find this book and its Companion Website of Web links and templates invaluable and convenient to use.

WHO SHOULD USE THIS BOOK?

This book offers a gateway for individuals who want to improve their instruction and the achievement of elementary-school-aged students by using the Internet's best resources. This book is written for use by the following types of individuals.

1. **Pre-service teachers** in elementary education programs who are enrolled in courses such as:
   - General methods
   - Curriculum and instruction
   - Introduction to educational technology
   - Introduction to education
   - Any of the specific content area methods courses, such as science, social studies, language arts, and mathematics
   - An internship
2. **In-service elementary school teachers** enrolled in graduate programs or professional development training in their school districts or who are, on a personal level, interested in further development of their skills.
3. **Parents** of children enrolled in elementary school and individuals who are home schooling.
4. **Curriculum specialists** in school districts for use in continuing education.

This book offers coverage of the best websites for standards, content, strategies, materials, and lesson plans selected by two full professors at a major university with one of the largest elementary education programs in the country. This book can be used as a supplement to a traditional text, as an organizing text for professors who prefer to develop their own "text packs," and as a resource when preparing curriculum.

WHY IS THIS BOOK NECESSARY?

After interviewing many elementary school teachers and having taught pre-service and in-service elementary school teachers for a number of years, we have concluded that a book that organizes the vast resources of the Internet into a format that matches how teachers think about their classroom and lesson plans and that only includes durable, authenticated websites would be a valuable asset to teachers. With the help of Merrill/Prentice Hall, we are bringing this book to you. And, because there are so many excellent websites and we wanted to minimize the costs of the book, we are offering **Bonus Website Links** on the Companion Website to this text. With this in mind and your support, we believe the purpose of the book will fulfill these goals.

WHAT ARE THE GOALS OF THE BOOK?

The goals of this text are to provide a new resource that

1. Explains the Internet and the PC and provides options and ideas on how to gather and catalog your Internet resources so that you can effectively infuse them into your teaching.

2. Provides connections to national and state accrediting and professional organizations' websites and standards for the subject fields that are taught in K–6 education.

3. Includes current Internet resources for basic skills, thinking skills, and information on a range of topics from parent-teacher conferences to at-risk students.

4. Organizes websites within each subject field taught by elementary school teachers based on how teachers organize their lesson planning:

   A. **National, professional organizations, and state standards and objectives** links provide information about standards and the content and related pedagogical approaches recommended through the professional organizations. In Chapter 7, Science and Technology, as an example, the National Science Teachers Association (NSTA) at **http://www.nsta.org/** and the Eisenhower National Clearinghouse at **http://www.enc.org/** are comprehensive sources on lesson plans, course materials, and information on science standards.

   B. **Content background information** for teachers. Because most elementary school teachers do not specialize (as do secondary school teachers) in a subject field, they often feel that they do not have the same level of background knowledge and expertise in the subject areas. This book provides links so that teachers can gain the background knowledge to develop lessons that use accurate and timely content with rich resources from the Internet. Gateway sites such as the WWW Virtual Library: History: United States at **http://vlib.iue.it/history/USA/** and specific sites such as The Nine Ten Planets at **http://www.nineplanets.org/** provide a convenient method to learn or relearn content.

C. **Lesson plans, strategies, and materials** will provide links to lesson plans and materials at learned societies such as the National Council for Social Studies (NCSS) and the National Council of Teachers of Mathematics (NCTM) and such organizations as National Geographic at **http://www.nationalgeographic.com/**, New York Public Television at **www.Thirteen.org**, and RubiStar High Plains Regional Technology in Education Consortium at **http://rubistar.4teachers.org/index.php**, where you can create rubrics online and, of course, ERIC and GEM, the Gateway to Educational Materials (see Chapter 2).

D. **Sites for use in the classroom or learning resource center with children,** such as the Anatomy of a Frog at **http://biology.about.com/library/blfrogmouth.htm** or virtual tours at the Latter Day Saints Home Schooling site at **http://ldshomeschoolinginca.org/vft.html**, offer K–6 students interactive opportunities to explore subject matter and develop academic skills.

We hope you agree that such a collection of website links will help you integrate the World Wide Web into your instruction and improve your students' learning skills.

HOW ARE THE GOALS ACHIEVED?

We achieve these goals by organizing the information from an unwieldy and constantly changing resource—the Internet—and providing:

1. Organized information by chapters and headings that make it easy for teachers to conveniently and quickly identify and locate the resources they need.

2. Concisely annotated links to sites for content, standards, lesson plans, and activities for use with elementary-school-aged students.

3. A contemporary approach to cataloging and saving lesson plans and resources that come from the Internet. (See Chapters 3 and 4, and on the Companion Website open **Lewis&Clark-CN.doc** for an example of a way to organize your lesson plans with Internet resources and **Classnotes-template.doc** for a template you can use.)

4. Criteria for you to use in selecting websites and, in particular, lesson plans on the Internet.

ACKNOWLEDGMENTS

We would like to thank the reviewers for their insightful comments and ideas. They are Elizabeth Brennan, St. Mary's College of California; Joyce W. Frazier, University of North Carolina, Charlotte; Honor Keirans, SSJ, Chestnut Hill College; Natalie Milman, George Washington University; Lindsay Ribaya, Lawton Chiles Elementary, Tampa; Kris Sloan, Texas A&M University; Gary L. Willhite, Southern Illinois University; and Cindy Wilson, Southwest Missouri State University.

Thank you for considering *The Elementary Teacher's Guide to the Best Resources on the Internet.* We hope it will make a significant difference in the quality of your instruction and your students' success.

Read Me First

The Internet is a remarkable resource for teachers. In 2001 the U.S. Department of Education reported that approximately 98 percent of schools have the capacity to support online initiatives. In the near future, U.S. schools will have achieved universal and high-speed access, and with that access, the potential for you to improve the learning experiences of your students is greatly enhanced. How to harness the power of the Internet, catalog and organize the resources for continued use, and strategically deploy these Web-based assets is the focus of this book.

THE FOCUS OF THE BOOK

The focal point of this text is the *annotated websites* that are organized into subject field chapters. When we interviewed our elementary school colleagues in preparation for this book, they suggested this structure because their planning starts with a single discipline (language arts, social studies, etc.) even if it is later expanded to support interdisciplinary or thematic teaching units. As teachers mentally organize for a lesson, they are choreographing **goals**, **strategies**, **content**, and **materials** into a lesson plan. The Internet provides sources for all these segments of planning and teaching, but—in only the short time the Internet has existed—sources have become varied in quality and are sometimes inaccurate. By providing you a compilation of reputable websites that have been reviewed and annotated, we hope to make your use of the Internet more effective and a more valuable part of your instruction. By focusing on exceptional websites and providing you with a brief description of each, we expect that you will be able to easily and quickly find the kinds of resources you need. We hope you will come to think of the authors as your "personal shopper" for Internet resources.

THE ORGANIZATION OF THE BOOK

The following brief description of the chapters is intended to assist you in making the most effective use of this book and its Companion Website at **www.prenhall.com/cruz**.

- Chapters 1 and 2 provide a basic overview of the Internet for use in elementary education and how to navigate the World Wide Web. In addition, important websites of a general nature such as ERIC and GEM are also annotated in these chapters.
- Chapters 3 and 4 offer practical strategies and criteria to select, integrate, and catalog Internet resources for your lesson planning and teaching and provide a number of elementary education gateway websites that are multidisciplinary.

- Chapter 5, Reading and Language Arts, includes the basic skills of reading, writing, and the expressive arts that have been the centerpiece of elementary language arts instruction for centuries, and their importance has been reemphasized with the passage of the *No Child Left Behind* legislation.

- Chapters 6 through 11 cover the subject fields of mathematics, science and technology, social studies, fine and performing arts, health and physical education, and world languages. These chapters are organized into categories based on your needs.
  - National, Professional Organizations and State Standards
  - Content Background Information
  - Lesson Plans, Strategies, and Materials
  - Sites for Use in the Classroom with Children

- Chapter 12 offers websites on parent-teacher relations, ELL students, learning styles, special education, and other topics that can serve as a foundation for your success in managing the complex interactions in your classroom and school.

- Chapters 13 and 14, our two "Tool Kits," identify resources especially helpful to teachers and students, respectively.

CRITERIA FOR SELECTION OF WEBSITES

Teachers should select websites for their use based on a number of criteria. For this text, the criteria were quality, credibility, and durability.

1. **Quality:** Each site was reviewed for the quality of the website and the relevance or significance of the information.

2. **Credibility:** There are no guarantees that content on the Internet is accurate. For Internet sites, like any information medium, the source is a major consideration. An emphasis was placed on sites whose sponsors have reputations for service to the public good, such as professional organizations, the Smithsonian, government organizations, and well-known institutions such as universities.

3. **Durability:** Content on the Internet is fluid. Because you will need to rely on specific sites for your work as a teacher, we gave priority to websites that are likely to be around for a long time and that are regularly updated.

With this in mind, we focused on what we call **gateway** websites for publication in the book. The websites we categorized as "gateways" are comprehensive; that is, they provide multiple links to resources created by their sponsors as well as resources by other sponsors. The additional **Bonus Links** located on the Companion Website will be of an equal quality and credibility. However, these websites are of such a nature that they are more limited in scope and often very specialized. They may not be as durable.

Contents

Note: Every effort has been made to provide accurate and current Internet information in this book. However, the Internet and information posted on it are constantly changing, so it is inevitable that some of the Internet addresses listed in this textbook will change.

CHAPTER 1

Understanding Internet Technology and Terminology

> ☞ **REMEMBER!**
> Visit the Companion Website at **www.prenhall.com/cruz** for links to each website in this book.

To make use of the resources of the Internet, you should become familiar with a number of key concepts and terms related to the Internet and computing technology. Although you may know some of this information, we hope our explanation applies to your role as a teacher in ways that make it more useful.

INTERNET HISTORY

The **Internet** resulted from **ARPANET**, a network of computers that the U.S. Department of Defense created in the late 1960s that could communicate with each other over existing land lines (telephone lines initially). Using the capabilities of the Internet, the **World Wide Web** (WWW) was invented in the early 1990s by Tim Berners-Lee. From the thousands of connections between the computers of the Internet, he wove the World Wide Web by creating the computer language and protocols to make the complex system manageable and usable for the general population. The idea was to develop a capacity that would make it easier to access and share resources found on computers at locations around the world. As of 2006, it has around 6.8 million **host computers** in the network. A school district, college, or museum (as examples) would use a host computer for its website, e-mail, and so on.

The World Wide Web provides users, such as teachers, with access to an array of **multimedia** information: text, graphics, moving pictures, and sounds, whether it is for commercial, educational, government, or personal use. The software to navigate the Internet, such as Microsoft Explorer and Netscape, and the publishing software, such as Microsoft's FrontPage and Macromedia's Dreamweaver, have developed so rapidly and become so consumer friendly that knowing how the Internet or your personal computer works has become like being able to explain how your refrigerator works. Most of us can't explain it technically and only care that it works almost all the time. However, knowing some key terms and ideas will help you better understand how your personal computer and the Internet make this new technology possible.

KEY TERMS OF THE INTERNET

The following are terms and underlying concepts about the Internet that you should become familiar with.

Hypertext. The defining characteristic of WWW services is the ability for you to travel from one document (image, video, or sound) that you are viewing on your computer screen to another document at another location anywhere in the world. As an example, at a university's **home page**, which is located on one **server** (a specialized type of computer that houses materials for availability on the WWW), you might see the link "**College of Education**," and when you click on it, it most probably sends you to another **server** on campus in the college of education building that displays the home page of the college of education. On the college of education home page, you may have text that says "U.S. Department of Education," and when you click on it, it takes you to a computer in Washington D.C. (although the server could be physically located anywhere) that has the home page of the Department of Education. These highlighted pieces of text have embedded network links, and this text is known as **hypertext**. Vannevar Bush first proposed the basics of hypertext in 1945. Tim Berners-Lee invented the World Wide Web in the 1990s by developing **HTML** (hypertext markup language, the computer language used to create Web pages of hypertext), **HTTP** (hypertext transfer protocol, the architecture of systems and codes that moves information on the servers), and **URLs** (uniform resource locators, the equivalent to a traditional street address).

Home Page. The first hypertext document displayed when you follow a link to a Web server is usually the home page.

Browser. The software you use to display and interact with a Web hypertext document; Microsoft Explorer as an example.

HTML (hypertext markup language). The encoding scheme used to format a Web document. The various HTML symbols define hypertext links, reference graphics files, and designate nontext items such as buttons and check boxes. Software such as FrontPage and Dreamweaver allows individuals to create websites without learning the HTML "language" just as word processing software translates millions of lines of computer code into the visual and easy-to-use software.

HTTP (hypertext transfer protocol). The protocol used by the Web to transfer hypertext documents and other **Net** (short for Internet) resources.

URL (uniform resource locator). A Web addressing scheme that spells out the exact location of the Net resource on another computer. Most URLs take the following form: **protocol://host.domain/directory/file.name**

The information on the Ph.D. program in social science education at the University of South Florida is at **http://www.coedu.usf.edu/main/departments/ seced/ssePhDintro.htm**

- *http* is a code that tells the software what protocol resource to use in retrieving the data.
- *www.coedu.usf.edu* is the host-domain, the domain name of the host computer where the resource resides.
- *main/departments/seced* are all directories like the folders on your personal computer and are used to organize and track materials by the people who create them.
- *ssePhDintro.htm* is the file and type of file, just like you would have a Microsoft Word file of your résumé on your computer, "smith resume.doc."

Domain Addresses. Internet addresses are, for the most part, based on **DNS**, the Domain Name System. The last part of an address can be used to denote either the type of institution or perhaps the country where the addressed computer is located. Some common institutional suffixes:

.org—Nonprofit organization (*e.g., NCSS.org*)

.com—Private company or corporation (*e.g., ibm.com*)

.gov—Government agency (*e.g., whitehouse.gov*)

.mil—Military installation (*e.g., gopher.nic.mil*)

.edu—Schools, school districts, universities (coedu.usf.edu)

If you would like to learn more about the Internet, the Library of Congress website at **http://lcweb2.loc.gov/learn/start/inres/gen/using.html** offers a **gateway** (the term *gateway* is used throughout this book to describe a website that is a comprehensive resource of links to information on its website and/or to other sites on a topic) to a broad range of information about the Internet.

At **webTeacher** at **http://www.webteacher.org/windows.html** there is a tutorial on the Internet designed with teachers in mind.

But ultimately, the best way to learn the Internet is to explore its various sites and features. The chapters in this text offer a wide range of websites related to elementary education. These World Wide Web resources will make a difference in the classroom experience of your students.

KEY TERMS OF YOUR PC

The term *personal computer* is used in this text to refer to either a **PC** (typically with a Windows operating system installed on a computer from manufacturers such as Gateway or Dell) or a **MAC/Apple**. As a teacher, you can use your personal computer resources and/or your school's computer resources to connect with the Internet and integrate the Net's resources with the capabilities of your personal or school computer. The teacher who has a computer at school and one at home (or a laptop to be used in both locations) that connects to printers and scanners can spend less time on everyday planning and administrative tasks and more time on creative endeavors essential to quality instruction. In many cases (check with your accountant!) your personal computer resources are tax deductible. The following descriptions should be of assistance to your participation in decisions regarding planning of technology in your school and purchasing a personal computer.

YOUR SCHOOL'S TECHNOLOGY CONFIGURATION

At the time of this publication, the ideal configuration for a school might be considered by many to include the following resources. Assuming a class size of 25 students, the school would provide each teacher/classroom a computer with an Internet connection, scanner, digital camera, printer, and a large monitor or a projector, and five computer stations with Internet connections for group work.

If there are also 25 stations with Internet connections in a computer laboratory or the learning resource center (**LRC**) that can be reserved, all 25 students could use a station at the same time during an assigned task. If the school is **networked** (all the computers are connected to each other and a server) with a website that supports e-mail and individual classroom or teachers' websites, the school can be said to provide a comprehensive platform of options for using technology to teach and perform the myriad of other tasks that make up a teacher's professional duties. **PDAs** (personal digital assistants) are becoming more commonplace. They are designed to be held in the hand and can house software such as Microsoft Word, e-mail, Internet wireless connections, and content software that might be tied to a textbook.

This level of technology may be different from what is at your school. Believers in the use of digital technology are alarmed by reports of computers stacked in corners and never used. Teachers point to antiquated equipment and the lack of a comprehensive platform as inhibiting their use of the technology.[1] Administrators complain of budget constraints and the difficulty of even keeping working light bulbs in overhead projectors. All of this is true.

---

[1]National Center for Educational Statistics (NCES). (2000). *Teachers' tools of the twenty-first century: A report on teachers' use of technology*. Washington, DC: U.S. Department of Education.

However, the promise of digital technology is too great for us not to overcome such problems. And progress is being made. Most public school teachers (84 percent) reported having at least one computer in their classrooms. Approximately half of the public school teachers who had computers or the Internet available in their schools used them for classroom instruction. Sixty-one percent of teachers assigned students to use these technologies for word processing or creating spreadsheets and about 50 percent assigned tasks requiring Internet research, drills, and solving problems and analyzing data.[2]

YOUR PC'S CONFIGURATION

Given the rapid changes in cost and technology, information (much less advice) on personal computer purchases is rapidly changing. The options for purchasing a personal computer (the hardware, operating system, and application software) can be mind boggling. One thing is for sure, personal computers and software have generally gotten less expensive and faster. The first question to be answered is usually "Will I buy a PC or a MAC/Apple?" This is largely a personal preference based on cost, performance, maintenance, and warranties. You can pay as little as $700 for a "low end" PC with a printer and scanner from a reputable company, and it should serve you well. For $1,000, a computer should be able to handle new technologies for a few years. In 2004, Apple offered the company's professional-level desktop, the G5, for about $1,799. At the publication time of this book, a comparable PC, the Dell Dimension 8300, with monitor and keyboard (not included with the MAC), retails for $1,050. Many universities and school districts have discount programs for the purchase of a computer for personal use and are worth checking into. Comparison shopping based on comparable memory, speed, warranty, and software can easily be accomplished on the Internet.

The following are some of the key terms to know and use in comparison shopping for computers. You could expect to have the following capabilities using the price tag of approximately $1,000 for a PC:

CPU at 3.2 **GHz** (the speed of the processor): The CPU (**central processing unit**) is the "brains" of the computer. Gigahertz refers to the speed. The higher the GHz, the faster and more expensive the computer.

RAM or "Memory" at 1 GB: **Random access memory** (RAM) or internal memory determines how much data can be handled in the fastest way at one time—the larger the better. **Cache** expands the amount of data that can be processed quickly.

Video and Sound Cards: These cards make sound and video possible and are essential.

Hard Drive at 160 GB (**gigabytes**): The second type of memory, the hard drive is the computer's electronic filing cabinet, and it stores the computer's

---

[2]Ibid.

operating system, files, programs, and documents. Data from the Internet and from the hard drive are moved to the RAM for manipulation.

CD-ROM Drive—Read/Write: Most new computers now come with a CD-ROM drive as standard equipment. At a minimum, you should have one that both creates (writes) and reads **CDs**. With CDs you can save more or seldom-used files should your hard drive become full. You should consider upgrading to a drive that also reads and writes **DVDs**.

56K Modem: This **dialup** mechanism comes with your computer and connects a computer through a phone line so the user can access the Internet. Like high-speed Internet service, you will usually pay a monthly connection fee.

High-Speed Internet Service: DSL from your telephone company or **Broadband** from a cable television company offer speeds that are roughly 70 times faster than dialup. The provider will supply a special high-speed external modem for your computer to access the Internet. A school's or university's connection would be a high-speed connection, and the dialup connection as the primary connection to home personal use is quickly giving way to DSL and cable broadband.

Printers: Printers can be either laser or inkjet and color or black and white. **Laser printers** produce documents using the same technology as a copy machine, whereas **inkjet printers** literally spray ink onto the page. Printer prices are relatively low because printer companies gain much of their income on the ink cartridges.

Software: It is not our intention to promote one company, but it is undeniable that Microsoft Office (**application software**) and Windows (the **operating system software**) with Explorer dominate the marketplace. Teachers also find that PowerPoint and Works by Microsoft are also particularly useful to their profession; see **http://office.microsoft.com/en-us/FX011433021033.aspx.**

 CHECK THEM OUT!

The Companion Website at **www.prenhall.com/cruz** has **Bonus Links** that are not included in the textbook!

CHAPTER 2

Elementary School Teachers' Uses of the Internet

> ☞ **REMEMBER!**
> Visit the Companion Website at **www.prenhall.com/cruz** for links to each website in this book.

Although the Internet's ability to carry e-mail and your school's or class's Web page to constituents and the public is a major use of the Internet (and will be discussed later in this chapter), the focus of this book is on instruction.

TEACHERS' THREE PRIMARY USES

Three primary types of assets can be found on the Internet or as software that can be placed on your PC without a connection to the Internet:

1. **Content background information sites** so you can learn more about a topic before you plan a lesson and teach it;
2. **Lesson plans, strategies, and class materials** developed by other teachers, organizations, and textbook companies for use in the elementary classroom setting; and
3. **Children's sites** for use with children in the classroom or the school's library or resource center.

For this reason, Chapters 5 through 10 will use these subdivisions to make it easier for you to find the resources on the Internet that will allow you to upgrade the quality of students' learning experience. However, many sites offer all of these kinds of assets and at times will lead to some duplication when we think it is important enough to report the sites in more than one category.

INTEGRATING INTERNET RESOURCES INTO YOUR TEACHING

Two basic approaches to integrating Internet resources into your instruction are the **infusion approach** and the **modified Internet lesson approach**.

The Infusion Approach

The **infusion approach** is where a teacher has an idea for a lesson plan and wants to *infuse* resources from the Internet into his or her lesson. Internet resources can be choreographed into the instruction in four ways:

1. **Content.** This would take the form of background information for the teacher, content to integrate into the lesson, or content to use with the children. Some examples would be:

   - The United States Civil War Center at **http://www.cwc.lsu.edu/ cwc/links/links6.htm** provides civil war diaries that graphically depict life in the 1860s.

   - Innerbody.com at **http://www.innerbody.com/htm/body.html** provides multiple images of the human anatomy.

   - Literature for children at **http://palmm.fcla.edu/juv/juvTitleList.html** has a collection of over 500 classic children's literary works that can be downloaded and reproduced.

   - Annenberg/CPB at **http://www.learner.org/** has free online videos that combine content and methods demonstrating how to teach elementary mathematics that is organized by topics.

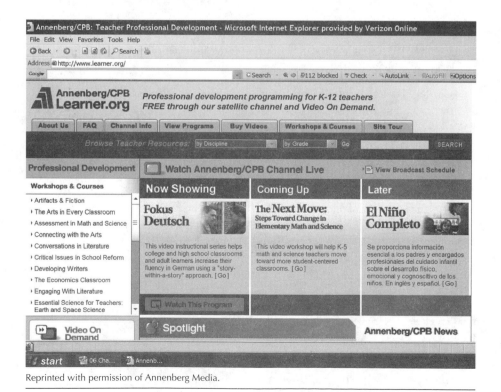

Reprinted with permission of Annenberg Media.

2. **A task or activity.** These are usually stand-alone experiences (as opposed to a comprehensive Internet lesson plan) that become part of the lesson. They may be downloadable paper-based tasks or interactive activities requiring students to complete the task at their desk or in groups at tables or to work at computer stations, or it is a teacher-centered activity using a large-screen monitor, as an example. Some examples are:

- Math.com at **http://www.math.com/students/practice.html** has practice problems in mathematics.

- Exploratorium at **http://www.exploratorium.edu/explore/handson.html** has activities in science.

- Colonial Williamsburg at **http://www.history.org/kids/visitUs/** is a dynamic site that integrates cartoon characters from history and pictures of Colonial Williamsburg where kids can learn about colonial life and take a virtual tour.

Reprinted with permission from the Colonial Williamsburg Foundation.

3. **Teaching materials.** From images that might be turned into transparencies to rubrics for projects, teachers can find free materials of high quality online. Some examples are:

- Google at **http://images.google.com/** allows you to search for images ranging from amebas to Lewis and Clark.

- At **http://gallery.yahoo.com/** you can search for names, places, things, and events. "Thumbnail" images are displayed of items such as Shakespeare, atoms, Newton, various kinds of cells, and Gettysburg, and these images can be turned into images for use in the classroom.

- National Geographic at **http://www.nationalgeographic.com/maps/** has maps for teaching geography.

- Teachervision at **http://www.teachervision.fen.com/page/6293.html** has examples and explanations of how a variety of graphic organizers (such as webs) can be used.

- Rubistar at **http://rubistar.4teachers.org/index.php** is a tool for creating rubrics online.

- American patriotic music can be downloaded or played from the Air Forces' website at **http://www2.acc.af.mil/music/patriotic/**.

- The University of Colorado has a website gateway to online science books at **http://spot.colorado.edu/~dubin/bookmarks/b/1240.html**, and the National Council for Social Studies offers a recommended list of notable trade books for children at **http://www.socialstudies.org/resources/notable/**.

4. **An extension**. This is when teachers move from one discipline to another or they integrate disciplines that often have a central theme (**thematic teaching**). As an example, the Betsy Ross website at **http://www.ushistory.org/betsy/** has a wealth of content for a lesson on the American Flag and an extension activity for art where students make a five-pointed star "in one snip" to be part of an American flag.

The Modified Internet Lesson Approach

The Internet has a large number of lesson plans that are of varying comprehensiveness, detail, and length. No matter how good a resource may appear, a teacher should rarely take a resource off the Internet "shelf" without modifying and improving it for use in her or his classroom and to meet local or state standards.

The **modified Internet lesson approach** is used when a teacher modifies and adapts a lesson plan found on the Internet to his or her students and circumstances. Internet lesson plans are different from activities and tasks because they tend to be comprehensive (i.e., they include goals or standards, content, a sequence to follow, tasks, materials, etc.) by having links to resources or downloadable attachments such as PDF files. At the National Endowment for the Humanities (NEH) EDSITEment website at **http://edsitement.neh.gov/view_lesson_plan.asp?id=387**, you can find short and multiday lesson plans that meet the criteria (see following section) for a high-quality lesson plan.

Although GEM (see Chapter 3) offers a gateway to resources for teachers, given the dynamic nature of the Internet, a search in any search engine can produce specific websites for lesson plans and for content to be used in a lesson that you create. As an example, Rutgers University has a comprehensive list of over 200 lesson plans and their activities for science at **http://www.physics.rutgers.edu/hex/visit/lesson/lesson_links1.html**, and the **Math Forum** at Drexel University at **http://mathforum.org/math.topics.html** has creative ideas and lesson plans that can be used in an elementary school classroom. **PE Central** at **http://www. pecentral.org/lessonideas/pelessonplans.html** has physical education activities, and **ArtsEdge** at **http://artsedge.kennedy-center.org/teach/les.cfm** has lesson plans for elementary school teachers in dance, music, theater, and visual arts.

SPONSORS OF INTERNET RESOURCES

Today's digital resources come from multiple sources.

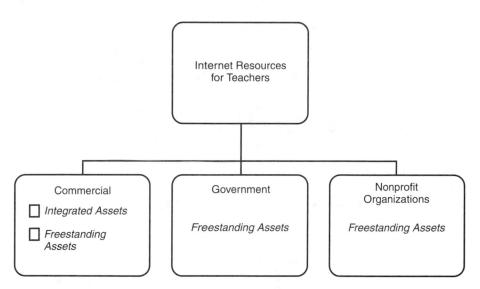

Integrated assets, the resources that come with a textbook, are frequently re-ferred to as **ancillary materials** and may include a teacher's edition of a textbook, worksheets, and so on. Publishers still provide ancillary materials in nondigital formats, but often these are becoming only those kinds of items that cannot be accessible via the Internet or a CD such as manipulatives, posters, and so on. These are often referred to as **courseware**. Many publishers now include websites (for example, **Scott Foresman** at **http://www.scottforesman.com**) that you have access to because your school might be using their textbook. These websites will often contain content background information sites; lesson plans, strategies, and class materials; and online children's activities. Typically these websites are copyrighted and have passwords to restrict use to only teachers in schools that have purchased the book.

Freestanding assets are independent of your textbook and may come on a CD or by way of the Internet. **ClassZone** developed by Houghton Mifflin at **http://www.classzone.com** offers resources geared to their elementary school textbooks, but often they can be used even if your school has not adopted the text. In some cases a website owner makes resources available for free in order to generate "hits" (this is when you go to a website; it records the number of people who log on) because that is a source of revenue from the advertisers it has displayed at the site. **Discovery School** at **http://school.discovery.com/lessonplans/** is such a site and has many resources for elementary school teachers. These kinds of assets can be retrieved at no cost, purchased over the Internet, or available for a fee or through membership. When there are no copyright restrictions, the resources that are available on the Internet fall into the **public domain**, and usually the website indicates its **Terms of Use**.

Government and **nonprofit organizations** seem to rarely have integrated assets. And their freestanding assets are generally available to the public at no cost. The **U.S. Treasury for Kids** at **http://www.ustreas.gov/kids** has resources appropriate for elementary school children from the history of coins to how savings bonds work.

Some nonprofit organizations include professional organizations such as the **National Science Teachers Association** at **http://www.nsta.org/** or **Education World** at **http://www.educationworld.com/**, which offers lesson plans, current topics, tips, and so on.

Reprinted with permission from Education World.

STAND-ALONE PC USES FOR TEACHERS

We access the Internet primarily through computers, but computers have both **stand-alone functions** (a grade book created with software on the personal computer) and **Internet functions** where the combination of hardware and software makes access and searching the Internet possible and integrates the capacities of both the computer and the Internet (saving favorites or copying or downloading course materials to your personal computer, as an example). The following are examples of assets that you can use to enhance your instruction.

Instructional Options

CDs and **DVDs** are the major vehicle for delivering non-Internet resources to PC users. It usually comes in the form of **content-specific CDs** (such as a CD on the human body that you can use with your personal computer). For a relatively small investment, freestanding **general-content CDs**, such as digital encyclopedias like *Compton's Interactive Encyclopedia*, *The Grolier Encyclopedia*, and *Encarta*, provide a wealth of background information and course materials without use of the Internet.

The content-specific courseware that comes on a CD that is integrated with the textbook by a publisher has been developed with consultants and tends to have a high degree of credibility and aesthetic quality. When selecting textbooks, the quality of software should be evaluated along with the book. A number of websites offer descriptions and evaluations of courseware and educational CDs. The California Instructional Technology Clearing House for the California public schools provides teachers' evaluations of courseware at **http://clearinghouse.k12.ca.us/** and is a good starting point for identifying and selecting educational CDs or courseware. Your learning resources coordinator may ask you for suggestions, or the PTA might have funds for teachers who want courseware for their classrooms.

Administrative Options

Administrative tasks are a necessary part of a teacher's life. **Application** or **"productivity" software** can make maintaining grades; communicating with parents, administrators, classroom visitors, and colleagues; and documenting interactions with students and parents less burdensome and time consuming. Teachers can use software such as Corel Word Perfect, Microsoft Office, and PowerPoint to create high-quality handouts and images as transparencies or for projection, as well as for administrative tasks.

Microsoft Works and AppleWorks are low-cost application software packages that combine a word processor, a database, and a spreadsheet into an integrated program. Besides letting you write correspondence, they allow you to create a grade book that adds and calculates averages and totals automatically. An address book created in the database can insert names or any other data elements into letters, so that parents receive personalized communications and status reports on their children. Tent cards for open houses can also be created with a database, as well as mailing labels and envelopes. A calendar for planning is one of many templates. One of the main advantages of such software is that it preserves a document to be used again, so that the teacher does not have to re-create it (see more about this in Chapter 3). An important advantage of using word processing programs is that the appearance of documents makes a positive statement about your professionalism.

E-mail can be an effective tool for communicating with parents about class-room activities, with students, and with other teachers. The same considerations that go into deciding whether to give parents your phone number apply to e-mail. Not all parents or students have home computers, so e-mail cannot be the only form of communication. Free e-mail service is available from **http://www.yahoo.com** and **http://www.hotmail.com.** However, most schools and school districts are now providing institutional e-mail addresses for their teachers and, if you are going to correspond with parents by e-mail, we would encourage you to use your district-sponsored e-mail address.

School and **classroom websites** are now being supported by school districts. A one-day seminar is sufficient for most teachers to learn the basic techniques of creating and maintaining a simple website. Listing homework, changes in planned curriculum, special events, lesson plan summaries, links for activities for parents to work with their children, and classroom rules on your website can further the aims of the classroom experience.

INTERNET SAFETY

Safety is a significant consideration for teachers who have their students use the Internet in school. It is always better to err on the side of caution. Teachers should always preview and prescribe sites to be used in lessons. Students should not be allowed to roam the Internet unsupervised. **Cyber Smart** at **http://www.cybersmartcurriculum.org/home/** offers a curriculum, lesson plans, and activity sheets by grade level that you can use to teach your students about safe use of the Internet, and **Microsoft** offers tips for parents at **http://www. microsoft.com/athome/security/children/parentsguide.mspx.**

Reprinted with permission from the CyberSmart Education Company.

Teachers need to follow three key rules in their classroom Internet use:

1. When using the Internet in presentations with children, the teacher should have previously previewed the site.
2. When students are working in groups or individually at computer stations on an activity designed by the teacher, for many assignments, the teacher should preview and save the sites to be used by the students.

3. When students are searching the Internet in groups or individually at the computer stations, the teacher must state the objectives to include going to sites that are appropriate to the goal and should be monitoring the students throughout the activity.

 CHECK THEM OUT!

The Companion Website at **www.prenhall.com/cruz** has **Bonus Links** that are not included in the textbook!

CHAPTER 3

Searching, Selecting, and Cataloging Internet Resources

> **☞ REMEMBER!**
> Visit the Companion Website at **www.prenhall.com/cruz** for links to each website in this book.

Prior to the blossoming of the Internet, teachers relied heavily on textbook packages (a textbook, teacher edition, ancillary materials [such as worksheets and transparencies]) and stand-alone (as opposed to being attached to the school's adopted textbook) commercial teacher materials that teachers would purchase at their own expense to plan their teaching. New thinking about teaching by experts and examples of lesson plans developed by other practicing teachers were published but were housed in journals only at universities, and thus, teachers were required to travel to academic libraries at usually great inconvenience for new ideas and resources. Teachers used the textbook chapters as the primary source of information on what content, thinking skills, and basic skills should be taught in the subject fields at each grade level. Textbooks often became the outer boundary of instruction, rather than just one resource. Rarely were comprehensive lesson plans included with the ancillary materials of the basal textbook. The best source for a lesson plan and its materials was typically a colleague who may have been willing to share his or her plan with you.

Today, the Internet can be used to overcome all of these shortcomings and indeed may be a necessity. Today, lesson planning needs to be driven by state standards in each subject field (see Chapter 4)—not a textbook. The new digital resources such as lesson plans and digital teaching materials need to be electronically saved, catalogued, and organized. Instruction can be greatly improved by learning others' approaches to instruction, and now you can access plans from teachers all over America (and anywhere in the world). And the most reputable resources can be retrieved conveniently from your classroom or home. Many Internet resources have been peer reviewed (meaning other experts have vouched for the authenticity and quality) or were developed by teams interested in advancing the quality of instruction at the elementary school level.

CRITERIA FOR SELECTING WEBSITES

A primary consideration is the validity of a website's assets. Some websites are inaccurate, biased, and purposefully misleading. This makes websites different from a textbook or courseware package by a national publisher, professional organization, or the government, which has typically undergone review and editing to ensure accuracy and a balanced presentation.

You can minimize the risks of invalid or inaccurate information or faulty strategies by focusing on websites sponsored by recognized and reputable institutions, such as museums, school districts, universities, libraries, and national organizations for teachers. Extensions identify types of institutions: .com (dot-com) is used for commercial enterprises, and the content of such sites is unregulated. The websites of educational institutions (.edu), nonprofit organizations (.org), and government institutions (.gov) are generally more reliable.

Beware of websites that appear to be legitimate. As an example, **http://www.whitehouse.gov** is the official site of the U.S. president's residence; **www.whitehouse.org** is a spoof of the official site.

Questions to Ask When Evaluating a Website

1. Are the goals and motives of the author and sponsor stated and clear?
2. Is the sponsor of the website known and credible?
3. Is the author of the materials on the website credible or an expert?
4. Do the aesthetics, graphics, content details, spelling, grammar, and so on indicate that the site has been thoughtfully organized and published?
5. Is the site dated?
6. Are the content and materials accurate, up to date, and usable?
7. Are the resources grade-appropriate?
8. Is advertising clearly labeled as such?
9. Is there a way for you to respond to the sponsor or author?
10. Can you count on the website to exist in the future?

These are the questions we asked ourselves as we searched the Internet for the resources that would be most helpful to you. One phenomena that we noticed was that some disciplines "were made" for the Internet. As an example, historical sites and historical figures are easily adaptable to the Internet medium. As a result, you can find multiple websites on almost any historical figure, place, or event, and social studies is one of the largest chapters. Science and mathematics did not necessarily have these ready-made resources, and many of their kinds of content are best presented in the more sophisticated interactive format of the Internet. The future looks very bright for all the disciplines as they take advantage of a new medium that by any standard is still in its infancy.

SEARCHING THE INTERNET

There are two primary approaches to finding resources on the Internet: **general searches** and **site-specific searches**.

General Search

With any search engine, such as Google or MSN, you can conduct detailed searches by using quotes and Booleans such as AND, OR, and NOT. As an example, if you insert *"long division" AND "lesson plan"* into a Google search box, you will generate over 600 websites ("hits"). It is, then, largely a matter of sifting through each site and assessing its quality and fit with your needs. Because it is a search of the Internet in general (as opposed to a site-specific search), it requires greater scrutiny, because it may not be from a credible or known source. The U.S. government, state agencies, national and state professional teacher organizations, textbook publishers, school districts and universities, and nonprofit organizations offer a degree of credibility, quality, and durability that teachers can usually rely on, because the lesson plan has typically undergone peer review (review by experts to insure their authenticity). Commercial websites such as Teacherworld and personal websites (a teacher who created some materials and posted it on the Web) offer many fine materials or lesson plans, but these resources may not have undergone any third-party review, and thus they cannot be assumed to have the same level of credibility.

Site-Specific Search

Chapters 5 through 11 of this book are largely dedicated to identifying websites by teaching field that you can use for resources in the classroom. The websites cited in those chapters pertain to such subjects as science or social studies. However, a number of multidiscipline sites cover elementary education in general, and three sites managed by the federal government should be a part of the resources you rely on.

MULTIDISCIPLINE SITES

Multidiscipline sites are not limited to any one teaching field and are usually organized with a search box and/or listings by subject field, grade level, or type of material (lesson plan, rubrics, etc.). The following are some of the sites we selected:

- The **Annenberg/CPB's Learner.org** website at **http://www.learner.org/index.html** offers online videos of teachers using best practices in classrooms with real students. You can select the discipline, subject, and grade level.
- The **Core Knowledge** website at **http://www.coreknowledge.org/CK/index.htm** has extensive lesson plans for all grade levels in all the subject fields.
- **Teachervision** at **http://www.teachervision.fen.com/** has multiple resources, including lesson plans, rubrics, and other materials.

Reprinted with permission from the Core Knowledge Foundation.

- The **National Endowment for the Humanities** maintains the EDSITEment website at **http://edsitement.neh.gov** with assets for all the humanities.
- **Discovery School** at **http://school.discovery.com/lessonplans** allows you to select materials by subject field and grade level.
- The **Lessons Plans Page** at **http://www.lessonplanspage.com/index.html** has over 2,500 activities; many are very brief but could be effective if redeveloped into a "real lesson plan" (see Chapter 4).
- New York Public Broadcasting's **Concepts to Classrooms** series at **http://www.thirteen.org/edonline/concept2class** has video demonstrating methods with teachers in elementary school classrooms.
- The **Smithsonian's** website at **http://www.si.edu** has resources that span the humanities through the sciences and has both a teachers' and a kids' section.

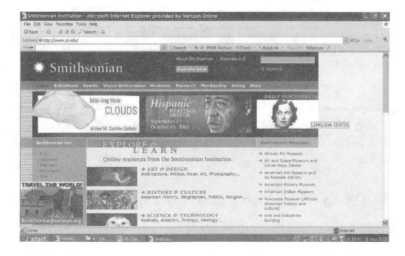

- **Education World** at **http://www.educationworld.com** is comprehensive with information on classroom rules, learning games, lesson plans, and more.
- **EdHelper** at **http://www.edhelper.com** requires a subscription and provides lessons, reading materials that are grade appropriate, worksheets, and assessments for multiple topics.
- **Awesomelibrary** at **http://www.awesomelibrary.org** has a large number of reviewed lesson plans gleamed from multiple sites that are organized by subject field and grade level.
- The **Critical Thinking Community** website at **http://criticalthinking.org/resources/TRK12-strategy-list.shtml** is dedicated to helping teachers convert typically "low level thinking" lessons to critical thinking lessons.

Reprinted with permission from the Foundation for Critical Thinking.

- **MiddleWeb.com** at **http://www.middleweb.com/CurrStrategies.html**, although dedicated to middle education, has many resources adaptable to elementary education.
- The **Curriculum Archive** at **http://www.buildingrainbows.com/CA/ca.home.php** is a collection of lesson plans by grade level, many of which offer thematic lesson planning opportunities.
- **Education Planet** at **http://www.educationplanet.com/** is a gateway to lesson plans and course materials catalogued by disciplines and more detailed categories.
- **Sites for Teachers** at **http://sitesforteachers.com/index.html** has hundreds of websites for teachers rated by popularity.

Reprinted with permission from Sites for Teachers.

The above sites focus primarily on instructional resources. You should go to Chapter 13, Teachers' Tool Kit, for additional websites that provide resources such as rubrics and tests.

THE MAJOR GOVERNMENT GATEWAYS

Three gateway government websites deserve special attention, because they span all the subject fields taught by elementary school teachers.

The Gateway to Educational Materials^{SM} (GEM)

GEM is a federally sponsored consortium effort to provide educators with quick and easy access to a substantial collection of educational materials (primarily lesson plans and teaching materials) found on various federal, state, university, nonprofit, and proprietary Internet sites. You can search by subject field, such as science, and by grade level by clicking on the "browse" keys or you can search for a specific topic with the search box, such as "solar system." GEM offers a breadth of resources that is found in few other sites.

Search Example. Open up your browser and go to **http://www.thegateway.org/browse**. Click on "*show*" next to "*Browse by subject*." As of 2006, there are over 12,000 science choices. Click on "*science*." In the right sidebar, scroll down to "*Grade Level*," and as you can see in the following screen shot, there are 3,854 items for third grade.

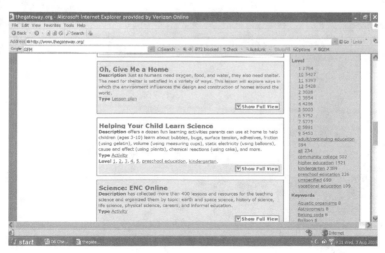

Using this screen shot, if you clicked on "*Lesson plan*" next to "*Type*" in the item "*Oh, Give me a Home*" (or any item listed), GEM will refresh the screen and give you a list of only lesson plans, not items characterized as "activity," and so on. By then clicking on third grade, again, in the right-hand box you will get only third grade science lesson plans.

For demonstration purposes, in the "Search the GEM Catalog" box type into the "FIND" box "Super AND Size" and select in the "IN" box, "Title" and press your enter key. A lesson plan titled "*Super Size Sun*" should appear. Click on "*Super Size Sun*" and a new page on your screen will open explaining how to teach the lesson. This lesson aims to demonstrate the size difference between the Sun and the Earth and includes the development of some mathematics skills (an extension) in an active learning format. It was developed by NASA, a respected organization.

Comparing Two Internet Lesson Plans. Go to the Core Knowledge website to view a lesson plan on the first Americans at **http://www.coreknowledge.org/CK/resrcs/lessons/02_Tech3_QuestEarliest.pdf**.

How would you evaluate this Internet lesson plan based on the criteria we have suggested? How would you evaluate "*Super Size Sun*"? Are they plans or activities, or somewhere in between? What is the quality? Would you find both useful? Are the originators of the plans reputable? Although this models the thinking process that you should go through when considering an Internet resource for use in your classroom, at the end of the search you have to decide whether it will ultimately help you assist your students achieve your goals as either an infused Internet resource or a modified Internet lesson plan.

ERIC (Educational Resources Information Center)

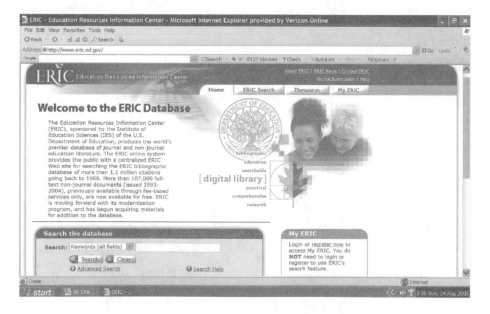

With over one million documents, **ERIC** is the academic index used by most educators to locate current research on education topics. It has a degree of credibility that is not true of the Internet in general because most entries are reprinted from academic journals, conference presentations, and national reports. Many of ERIC's documents are **full-text** documents, which means the entire document can be retrieved online as a **PDF** (portable document format). The goal is to eventually have all documents available as full-text, online PDF files. In the past, teachers were forced to spend endless hours in the library and at a microfilm machine to find current and classic ideas on how to teach in new ways; now we have the Internet.

Go to **http://www.eric.ed.gov**. A page like the screen shot on page 22 will be displayed. Select "Advanced Search." You will see that, when searching for documents based on a title, author, or keyword, you can request to view only those documents that are already available as full-text documents. Keep in mind that many of the best articles are not yet available online.

What Works Clearinghouse

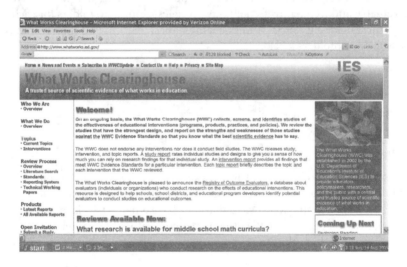

A new initiative being implemented as a result of the *No Child Left Behind legislation* is the **What Works Clearinghouse** (WWC) at **http://www.whatworks.ed.gov**. The What Works Clearinghouse was established by the U.S. Department of Education's Institute of Education Sciences to provide educators, policymakers, and the public with a central source of scientific evidence of what works in education. Like ERIC, it houses publications about education; however, a major difference is that it limits its publications to reviews of scientific evidence of the effectiveness of replicable educational interventions (for example, programs, practices, products, or policies) that promise to improve student outcomes.

DOWNLOADING AND CATALOGING RESOURCES

You have the option of saving website addresses such as GEM **http://www. thegateway.org** or the lesson plan "*Super Size Sun*" **http://www.nasaexplores.com/ show_k4_teacher_st.php?id=030109134411** into your Favorites folder of your browser. We believe this to be the minimum you should do. You should consider also saving a document such as "*Super Size Sun*" by copying its contents into a Word document and saving it to your hard drive. You should consider downloading and saving materials to your PC's hard drive because a lesson plan such as "*Super Size Sun*" may be deleted by NASA or NASA may change the structure of its website, making it difficult to find again. One of the new challenges presented by the volume of materials available to teachers by way of the Internet is the problem of keeping track of your materials, documents, and websites. The following are some ideas on how to manage your newly found resources.

Internet Folders

In your browser (we will use *Explorer* as our example) is the "**Favorites**" folder. You can add links to your Favorites and organize them into folders that will help you track valuable and frequently used links. We suggest setting up folders for each broad subject field (e.g., social studies, mathematics, science) and then within each of those, have subfolders labeled

- Standards
- Background (for background information for the teacher)
- Lesson Plans
- Course Materials (such as rubrics, handouts)
- Online Activities

By saving websites into these Favorites subfolders, you will make your work easier by keeping them organized and catalogued. Through the "Organize" feature of Favorites, you can rename websites so that they have a name that is more meaningful to you, and you can change the order in which they appear, so that you can put your most favorite sites at the top.

Retrieving Information, Documents, and Images

Most information on the Internet can be downloaded by copying and pasting into a Microsoft Word document, downloading an MS Word or PDF document, or clicking on an image, at which time the website will offer you the option to save the image to your PC as an image file. In the case of images, you can also use the "Print Screen" key function. If while you have a page on your screen displayed from the Internet, you press Print Screen, it will capture the entire image that is on the screen and save it temporarily for you to save in an MS Word document, as an example. Once captured by pressing the Print Screen key, you would open a new MS Word document, paste the image into the document, and then use the editor to crop and resize the image to meet your needs. This feature allows you to capture just about any image that appears on the Internet. It is how we captured the images from home pages for this textbook.

We hope the ideas in this chapter will assist you in making the most of the assets found on the World Wide Web for your classroom. The next chapter is intended to assist you in organizing, cataloging, and choreographing these new assets into your lesson planning.

 CHECK THEM OUT!
The Companion Website at **www.prenhall.com/cruz** has **Bonus Links** that are not included in the textbook!

CHAPTER 4

Standards-Based Lesson Planning with the Internet

> **☞ REMEMBER!**
> Visit the Companion Website at **www.prenhall.com/cruz** for links to each website in this book.

When selecting Internet lesson plans from either general searches or site-specific searches, you should consider several indicators of a well-developed plan. And even the best plans should be modified to meet your students' needs and your state's standards.

CRITERIA FOR SELECTING INTERNET LESSON PLANS

The criteria you should use for selecting Internet lesson plans are the following:

1. **Standards.** Is the plan tied to national or state standards?
2. **Instructional Sequence.** Is there a clear and detailed explanation of the sequence of the instruction? (See ClassNotes later in this chapter.)
3. **Rigor.** Does the plan challenge the students with tasks and activities that require critical thinking and self-discipline?
4. **Creativity.** Does the plan creatively engage the students with
   a. opportunities to develop skills and critical thinking,
   b. variety of strategies, and
   c. meaningful, grade-appropriate content?
5. **Resources.** Are there resources, such as well-crafted handouts or links to other high-quality websites?
6. **Evaluation.** Does the plan have an evaluation component?

The extent to which something on the Internet that is *called* a lesson plan actually *is* a lesson plan—rather than an activity or task—is based largely on how many of the above six components are found in the plan. The extent to which it is evaluated as excellent depends on the quality of the components. As discussed in

Chapter 3, the blossoming of the Internet has changed the opportunities to significantly improve the lesson plans we use to teach elementary school students. The accountability aspects of the "standards movement" have given even greater impetus to the need to use Internet resources. States that fail to meet expectations can lose federal funding, and schools that fail to meet state expectations can be closed. Teachers are on the front lines and, arguably, feeling more pressure to have their students succeed than anytime in the history of American education.

NATIONAL STANDARDS

Standards-based education is a relatively new phenomenon in education. It has many goals, not the least of which is to develop more uniform expectations for what is to be learned throughout the United States and to measure in some uniform way the success of students as they progress through the schools.

Although the standards movement predates President George W. Bush's January 8, 2002 signing into law the **No Child Left Behind Act of 2001 (NCLB)**, NCLB places the movement in a national context with a national impetus. It redefines the federal role in elementary education and is intended to close the achievement gap between disadvantaged or minority students and their peers in both general and discipline specific literacy. NCLB, more than any other legislation in American history, moves the United States closer to a national curriculum by mandating that states establish standards and measure students' success at meeting those standards. To define those standards, the states have relied on the guidelines in NCLB and the professional organizations (the websites for these organizations and their standards are listed at the beginning of Chapters 5 through 11).

The following two articles provide an analysis of NCLB and are available online through the **Education Resource Information Center** (typically referred to as ERIC) at **http://www.eric.ed.gov**, a major source of research in education.

- ED477723 *Implications of the No Child Left Behind Act of 2001 for Teacher Education.* ERIC Digest. Trahan, Christopher, 2002.

- ED478248 *The Mandate To Help Low-Performing Schools.* ERIC Digest. Lashway, Larry, 2003.

In addition to the above analyses, there are two key sources about how well American students are doing in school that are available on the Internet. One, the **Nation's Report Card** at **http://nces.ed.gov/nationsreportcard/**, provides national and comparative assessment data on students' knowledge.

Two, the Organization for Economic Co-operation and Development's (OECD) **Programme for International Student Assessment** at **http://www.pisa.oecd.org/document/55/0.2340.en_32252351_32236173_33917303_1_1_1_1.00.html**, provides comparative data on high school students' performance from an international perspective.

PROFESSIONAL ORGANIZATIONS' STANDARDS

The movement to a more uniform curriculum evidenced in the No Child Left Behind legislation also motivated the professional organizations for each of the teaching fields (see Chapters 5 through 11) to develop standards and to provide resources such as lesson plans and materials through the Internet to achieve those standards. To comply with NCLB, most states have adopted and modified the standards recommended by each discipline's professional organization. As a result, the math, reading and writing skills, and knowledge (content and skills) unique to each discipline that you will likely be expected to achieve with your students due to NCLB were most probably defined or heavily influenced by the national associations.

The following website links are related to curriculum and instruction, *in general*, as are those in Chapters 3, 12, and 13, as opposed to those organizations supporting specific disciplines (see Chapters 5 through 11). Many of these sites are multisubject websites (i.e., they have lesson plans and materials that support all the disciplines).

General Professional Organizations

- Association for Childhood Education International
  http://www.acei.org/
- National Association for the Education of Young Children
  http://www.naeyc.org/

Reprinted with permission from the National Association for the Education of Young Children.

- National Education Association
  http://www.nea.org/
- Association for Supervision and Curriculum Development
  www.ascd.org
- American Association of School Administrators
  http://www.aasa.org/

STATE STANDARDS

Your state standards can be found at **http://edstandards.org/Standards.html** or **http://www.aligntoachieve.org/AchievePhaseII/basic-search.cfm.**

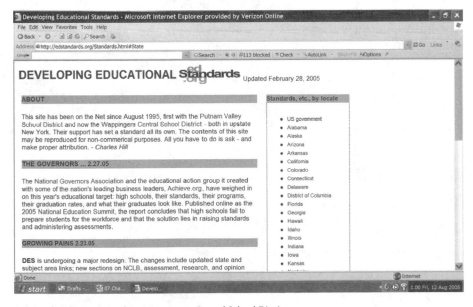

Reprinted with permission from Wappingers Central School District.

In the final analysis, your state will formulate and set the standards you are expected to achieve in your classroom. The two dominant approaches used to determine whether the standards are being met are:

1. **High-stakes testing**, which typically uses a point-in-time approach by using a paper-pencil test to determine skills such as reading, mathematics, and critical thinking. Some states at the elementary school level test for content in such fields as social studies and science.

2. **Lesson plans tied to state standards** in specific subject areas require teachers to indicate what specific state standard is being met by the lesson plan. The assumption is that *every* student will acquire the skill or knowledge prescribed in the standard upon completion of the lesson plan. It is also expected that through these subject-specific lesson plans students should also gain the kinds of general basic skills assessed in high-stakes testing.

Excellent instruction and committed families have a great impact on how well individual students succeed when measured by both approaches. The focus of this chapter is on lesson plans and the teacher's integration of the Internet into those plans to achieve standards.

STANDARDS-BASED LESSON PLANNING

In Chapter 3, we explained the different ways Internet resources can be used to improve lesson plans. Planning begins with a state standard, and how much documentation will be required of you varies greatly from state to state and school to school. In mathematics for the third grade, as an example, the state of Texas indicates 17 standards that should be achieved (see **http://www.tea.state.tx.us/teks/grade/Third_grade.pdf**). The following are the first two.

1. Number, operation, and quantitative reasoning. The student uses place value to communicate about increasingly large whole numbers in verbal and written form, including money. The student is expected to:
   a. use place value to read, write (in symbols and words), and describe the value of whole numbers through 999,999;
   b. use place value to compare and order whole numbers through 9,999; and
   c. determine the value of a collection of coins and bills.

2. Number, operation, and quantitative reasoning. The student uses fraction names and symbols to describe fractional parts of whole objects or sets of objects. The student is expected to:
   a. construct concrete models of fractions;
   b. compare fractional parts of whole objects or sets of objects in a problem situation using concrete models;

c. use fraction names and symbols to describe fractional parts of whole objects or sets of objects with denominators of 12 or less; and

d. construct concrete models of equivalent fractions for fractional parts of whole objects.

The level of detail provided by each state can vary greatly. However, in a system like the one in Texas, teachers can be expected to indicate a standard in their lesson plan that is to be achieved by the lesson, such as 2(a) above. These kinds of standards are often used as a replacement for objectives in lesson planning. You should go to **http://edstandards.org/Standards.html** and compare the approach in Texas to how your state defines its standards.

For many teachers, once they are familiar with the standards that they will be expected to achieve for their grade level during the upcoming year, the next step is to plan the **scope and sequence** for the year. The **scope** (the content and skill that are to be learned based on the standards) and **sequence** (the order in which the content and skills are to be learned) should be familiar to most future and current elementary school teachers in that it involves creating a calendar for the year of what you will teach each month, week, and day. If you go to MS Word and select New Document and then select Templates on Office Online, there is a calendar template of months and days that is ideal for this purpose.

The scope and sequence is the precursor to the daily or multiday lesson plan for each subject. Depending on the detail and how measurable the standard or benchmark is in your state, you may have to define more precisely what you expect students to be able to do to achieve the standard. Many teachers prefer to create that greater detail with the **behavioral objectives** approach based on Bloom's *Taxonomy of Educational Objectives.*[1] Go to Teacherworld's listing of **action verbs** at **http://teacherworld.com/potactionverbs.html** and the **ABCD method** at **http://teacherworld.com/potslo.html**. Combined, these have frequently been used to define expectations with measurable outcomes.

CATALOGING INTERNET AND PC RESOURCES

The new technology allows you to download lessons, materials, and activities developed by practitioners, publishers, and organizations from across the country to be choreographed into your lesson plans for your students. However, one of the new challenges presented by the volume of materials available on the Internet is the problem of keeping track of your materials, documents, and websites. By carefully organizing and cataloging your resources, you will be in a much better position to improve the quality of your instruction by being able to conveniently modify and add resources to lesson plans used one year before using the plan again the next year. The following are some ideas, in addition to the organization of the Favorites folders recommended in Chapter 3, on how to manage your newly found resources.

---

[1] Bloom, B. (1956). *Taxonomy of educational objectives: Handbook 1: Cognitive domain.* New York: David McKay.

Personal Computer Folders

We recommend a similar format for your folders created on your personal computer and saved in your **My Documents** folder as you did for the Favorites folder in your browser (see Chapter 3). For documents you need for instruction, we suggest—at a minimum—a folder named for each subject (science, social studies, etc.) and subfolders named:

- Background (for background information for the teacher)
- Lesson Plans
- Course Materials (such as rubrics, handouts)

You may want to go one step further. Using the American Revolution and Lewis and Clark Expedition in social studies as examples, you would organize your folders as such:

Social Studies
    American Revolution
        Background
        Lesson Plans
        Course Materials
    Lewis and Clark
        Background
        Lesson Plans
        Course Materials
  Etc.

The Background, Lesson Plans, and Course Materials folders also mimic the organization of this textbook. Consistent criteria and nomenclature should be used for placing documents in these folders for ease of future use, and we suggest you consider something like the following.

Background Folder. These would be documents having to do with background information for you about the pedagogical content knowledge of the subject. You will find downloadable PDF documents at **Education Resource Information Center** at **http://www.eric.ed.gov/** on methods and content that you can save to this folder, rather than having to go back to the Internet to retrieve them each time. On pages at various websites, you can save the Web address or highlight and copy information, and paste it into a word processing document, and save it to this folder. Using the Lewis and Clark example, at **PBS** at **http://www.pbs.org/lewisandclark/**, you will find information that you could use to develop a greater understanding of the content as well as maps, diaries, and so on that could be placed in the Lewis and Clark folder. Saving such information to your computer is important, because sometimes websites change and what you found previously may no longer be at the site the next time you visit the address. If you cut and paste background information into a Word document, you would want to give it a meaningful name (a name that you can easily recognize), such as **Lewis&Clark Background-W.doc** (where **W** equals website material, as opposed to **B** for a book, etc.). You should also copy and paste the Web address into the document to keep track of the source. In addition, you will find documents in a PDF, Word, or Excel format at websites that you can download. In this case as well, you will want to create a meaningful file name and use **W** to designate the type of source of the information as well.

Lesson Plans Folder. Lesson plans in PDF, HTML, and .doc formats can be downloaded from the Internet. You should make sure that the names are meaningful, or change them as well, prior to saving the document. Using the Lewis and Clark expedition as an example, **GEM** has 15 resources for third grade on this topic, ranging from a focus on Sacagawea on the American dollar to maps to lesson plans covering the Lewis and Clark expedition. The National Endowment for the Humanities EDSITEment website at **http://edsitement.neh.gov/** has 10 lesson plans related to Lewis and Clark. For the lesson plan, we also suggest adding the **Lewis&Clark Lesson Plan-W.doc** so you can distinguish these lesson plans from ones you create from scratch. For lesson plans you create and infuse Internet resources into, you could include **CN for ClassNotes** in the file name (see Class Notes later in this chapter) as opposed to **W**.

Course Materials Folder. Course materials are the kinds of documents you plan to use in class during instruction such as rubrics, graphic organizers, templates, examples, tests, and paper versions of transparencies, and images, which may be in GIF, JPEG formats, and so on. You should develop a nomenclature for these as well. Using a lesson on the Lewis and Clark expedition as an example, the following offers a model for naming and organizing a variety of documents.

- **Lewis&Clark-test.doc** would be a test; if more than one test, you could have test1, test2, and so on;
- **Lewis&Clark-map of Sioux nation.doc** would be a map saved in an MS word document; and
- **Lewis&Clark-picture of Clark.jpg** would be a JPG image. Our personal preference for images is to paste them into a Word document and, in this case, name it **Lewis&Clark-image of Clark.doc** because the Word picture editor can be used to size the image within the document for ease of printing as a transparency.

With this kind of organization of your electronic resources, you can keep track of your electronically stored files. Linking them together—that is, across folders—can be accomplished in how you organize and maintain the notes you will use in class to teach your students. One model is the **ClassNotes**[2] approach, which is effec-

---

[2]Duplass, J. A. (2006). *Middle and high school teaching: Methods, standards & best practices.* Boston, MA: Houghton Mifflin.

tive because this is intended to be the actual document a teacher uses during the instruction. This model should give you some ideas for the development of a specific model that works for you.

CLASSNOTES

For your lesson plans, we suggest you consider the three-column **ClassNotes** approach as a way of choreographing your instruction and integrating and linking all of your resources. On the Companion Website for this textbook is **ClassNotes-Template.doc**, a Word file providing the three-column format, and **Lewis&Clark-CN.doc**, which provides an extended example of ClassNotes for a Lewis and Clark expedition lesson.

ClassNotes		
Teacher Background Resources		
Standards		
Objectives		
Instructional Sequence, Strategies, & Tasks	**Teacher Talk & Content: Facts/Concepts/Big Ideas**	**Course Materials**
Attention Getter		
Review		
Content Presentation		
Practice		
Evaluation		

1. *In the first column*, you sequence the planned instruction into a series of steps. You have probably been exposed to many models in a methods class, such as Madeline Hunter's *Mastery Learning*[3] method; Robert Gagne's *Nine Events of Instruction* model;[4] Merrill's *First Principles of Instruction*;[5] and Gagnon and

---

[3]Hunter, M. (1982). *Mastery teaching*. Thousand Oaks, CA: Corwin Press.
[4]Gagne R. M. (1965). *The conditions of learning*. New York: Hold, Rinehart and Winston.
[5]Merrill, M. D. (2002). First principles of instruction. *Educational Technology Research and Development* 50(3), 43–59.

Collay's *Designing for Learning: Six Elements in Constructivist Classrooms*[6] The steps listed in the ClassNotes are generally accepted as part of the instructional process. The items listed in columns two and three that are associated with each step are kept parallel to the step. So if you used a part-to-whole[7] explanation as part of a content presentation, that term would be listed in the first column under Content Presentation. The strategies you plan to use, such as discussion, type of reading approach, types of lectures and group activities, comparing and contrasting, summarizing, hypothesizing, questioning, and structures, would appear under these headings to help you recall how you planned to deliver the information or experience. And if you used an image of Lewis and Clark on an overhead projector, as an example, as part of your attention getter, it would appear in the third column in the same row as Attention Getter.

2. *In the second column,* you sequence the content you plan to use during instruction. In this column, you would include content and skills to be acquired. Rather than detailing the content in this document, you may indicate and attach a copy of **Lewis&Clark-Content-W.doc** from our earlier example so you know what to print out and review in advance to teaching the lesson.

3. *In the third column,* you indicate the course materials, such as a drawing of planned board work, pages from the basal text, Internet sites, worksheets, and graphic organizers, that you plan to use in the order you plan to use them during the steps listed in the first column.

   a. Planned Internet resources are identified by inserting the website from your Favorites folder into the column and related row. As an example, an interactive map of the Lewis and Clark expedition territory that you might use in class as an online activity appears at **http://www.pbs.org/lewisandclark/trailmap/index.html**; it cannot be saved to your hard drive and therefore would be inserted as a link.

   b. Planned resources from your personal computer folders are catalogued by typing in the name of the document that is in your course materials folder. As an example, **Lewis&Clark-test.doc** would be a test on a Lewis and Clark lesson.

By developing a consistent pattern such as this, with the topic first and then the item type, all documents will appear alphabetically and grouped together by name within a folder. If you were to put "test" first, all tests would be grouped together when they appear in the MS Word Open Dialogue box or in the Folder Open box.

This ClassNotes format and cataloging nomenclature can easily be adjusted to suit your personal preferences for organization and style. But with the volume of materials on the Internet, it is wise to catalog your Internet resources and link them

---

[6]Gagnon, G. W., & Collay, M. (2001). *Designing for learning: Six elements in constructivist classrooms.* ERIC Document Reproduction Service No. ED451136.
[7]Duplass, J. A.(2006). *Middle and high school teaching: Methods, standards & best practices.* Boston, MA: Houghton Mifflin.

to your ClassNotes in a way that will make them easy to retrieve in the years to come.

On the Companion Website for this book is a Word document of a Lewis and Clark lesson plan using the ClassNotes approach and a template should you decide to use this strategy.

 CHECK THEM OUT!

The Companion Website at **www.prenhall.com/cruz** has **Bonus Links** that are not included in the textbook!

CHAPTER 5

Reading and Language Arts

Many educators would argue that reading and language arts are at the core of the elementary school curriculum. There is no doubt that these skills are essential for all the other academic areas. Fortunately, the Internet offers a myriad of resources, teaching ideas, and student-friendly sites that support quality language arts instruction.

The following professional organizations, journals, and standards play an essential role in language arts and reading education and the development of your teacher practices.

The National Council of Teachers of English (NCTE)

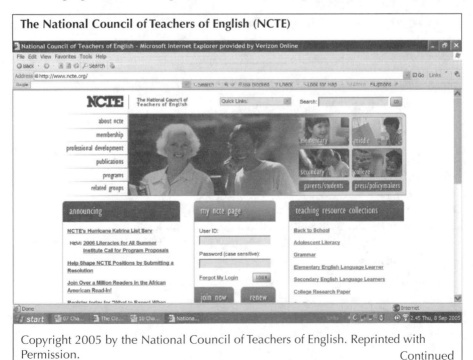

Copyright 2005 by the National Council of Teachers of English. Reprinted with Permission.

Continued

National Organizations and Standards on the Internet

Professional Organizations for Teachers of Language Arts

The National Council of Teachers of English
http://www.ncte.org/

International Reading Association
http://www.reading.org/

National Communication Association
http://www.natcom.org/

Related Organizations

The American Communication Association
http://www.americancomm.org/

The Academy of American Poets
http://www.poets.org/

American Comparative Literature Association
http://www.acla.org/

The American Folklore Society
http://www.afsnet.org/

The American Literature Association
http://www.calstatela.edu/academic/english/ala2/index.html

Association of Literary Scholars and Critics
http://www.bu.edu/literary/

Modern Language Association
http://www.mla.org/

American Forensics Association
http://www.americanforensics.org

Speech, Debate, and Theatre Association
http://www.nfhs.org/sdta/about_sdta.htm

National and State Standards

The National Standards for English Language Arts were developed by NCTE and IRA; see http://www.ncte.org/about/over/standards/110846.htm.
The **National Standards and Competencies for Speaking, Listening, and Media Literacy** can be found at http://www.natcom.org/Instruction/K-12/K12stdspr.htm.
INTASC Standards for English Teacher Education are in development; go to http://www.ccsso.org. Your **state standards** can be found at http://edstandards.org/Standards.html or http://www.aligntoachieve.org/AchievePhaseII/basic-search.cfm.

ERIC and GEM

ERIC, http://www.eric.ed.gov (see Chapter 3), has almost 8,000 online articles; search for "language arts" OR reading AND "elementary education".

GEM, http://www.thegateway.org/browse (see Chapter 3), has over 8,000 possible lesson plans in language arts for use at the elementary school level.

Reading and Language Arts

Content Background Information

Reading Comprehension Instructional Strategies

http://www.indiana.edu/~reading/ieo/bcata.html

This comprehensive site is intended to provide resources on reading comprehension instructional strategies for the elementary level. They were assembled from the World Wide Web, the ERIC database, and a variety of other bibliographic resources. There is information on whole language vs. phonics, use of graphic organizers, ability grouping, and so on.

Big Dog's Grammar

http://aliscot.com/bigdog/

Billed as a "bare bones guide to English," this Web resource plainly breaks down the parts of speech, modifiers, consistency rules, and parallel structure, among other things. The MLA Quick Guide is a handy resource with FAQs and easy-to-understand explanations of the rules.

The Children's Literature Web Guide

http://www.ucalgary.ca/~dkbrown/

The Children's Literature Web Guide gathers together and categorizes the growing number of Internet resources related to books for children and young adults. The information is organized into categories such as resources for teachers, parents, storytellers, award-winning books, and so on.

Carol Hurst's Children's Literature Site

http://www.carolhurst.com/toc.html

This exhaustive list of children's books can be searched by author, title, curriculum area, or grade level. Each book is summarized and reviewed professionally.

Citation Styles

http://www.bedfordstmartins.com/online/citex.html

This website explains each of the main citation styles (APA, MLA, Chicago, and CBE) and provides examples of each. Links to other online citation guides are also provided.

English-Zone.com

http://english-zone.com/index.php

A comprehensive website that provides detailed information about topics such as grammar, vocabulary, idioms, and communication skills. The Teacher Zone offers rubrics, in-class activities, and printable worksheets.

Great Writers

http://www.xs4all.nl/~pwessel/writers.html

This website lists literary prize winners and biographical information on a wide range of authors (arranged alphabetically). Many of the links take you to authors' home pages that offer even more information and resources.

Internet Public Library

http://www.ipl.org/div/litcrit

The IPL offers critical reviews of many works of literature. Users can browse by time period, country of authors' origin, authors' names, and titles.

Learning to Read

http://toread.com

This clearinghouse on reading research provides educators with the latest information on the reading process. Models of reading, developments in literacy, and professional materials and research are all reviewed on this website.

Project Gutenberg

http://www.gutenberg.org

Project Gutenberg provides over 15,000 free electronic books on the Internet. Most of the collection is older literary works that are in the public domain in the United States, so all of them may be freely downloaded, printed, and used in the classroom. Books such as *The Adventures of Huckleberry Finn* and *Voyages of Dr. Doolittle* can be accessed. Audio books, music, and images are also available.

Lesson Plans, Strategies, and Materials

American Folklore

http://www.americanfolklore.net/index.html

Among the many types of American folklore found on this site, teachers can access traditional American folktales, Native American myths and legends, tall tales, weather folklore, and ghost stories from across the United States.

The Children's Literature Web Guide

http://www.ucalgary.ca/%7Edkbrown

Great collection of children's book award lists, teaching ideas for children's books, and online book discussion groups. The Doucette Index functions as a search engine that enables users to access K-12 literature-based teaching ideas.

Kathy Schrock's Guide for Educators: Literature and Language Arts

http:// school.discovery.com/schrockguide/arts/artlit.html

A comprehensive gateway site to the best teaching resources on the Internet. Users can access literature activities, grammar and style guides, and poetry indexes.

Multicultural Resources for Children

http://falcon.jmu.edu/~ramseyil/ multipub.htm

In addition to articles on how to use multicultural reading resources in the classroom, there is an extensive listing of books with multicultural themes. The annotated bibliographies arranged by culture/ethnicity are particularly useful.

Online Children's Stories

http://www.ucalgary.ca/~dkbrown/stories.html

A nice collection of classics, folklore, and contemporary writing for children. There is also a Readers' Theatre section and writings by children.

Read Write Think

http://www.readwritethink.org/

An excellent collection of K-12 lesson plans, Web resources, and student materials. Teaching ideas can be searched by themes and grade levels. The lesson plan page is annotated with abstracts of each lesson and intended grade range. The Student Materials Index offers online tools and organizers for student work.

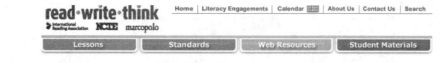

Reprinted with permission from Read Write Think.

Reading Rainbow

http://gpn.unl.edu/rainbow

In connection with the popular TV show *Reading Rainbow*, this website provides book lists, links to lessons and standards, and a host of library resources.

SmartBooks

http://www.k-state.edu/smartbooks/

This site has a large number of mathematics lesson plans by grade level, all of which are launched with a children's book. Students develop critical reading and problem-solving skills while enjoying age-appropriate literature.

Songs for Teaching: Language Arts

http://www.songsforteaching.com/reading.htm

This innovative site features lyrics and sound clips for songs that can teach about the parts of speech, reading comprehension, and vocabulary building. Young children will especially enjoy the nursery rhymes and twists on classic literature.

Starfall

http://www.starfall.com

Short stories that concentrate on a vowel or blend sound. By clicking on a word, help is given. Primarily designed for first grade, also useful for pre-kindergarten, kindergarten, and second grade.

The Teacher's Desk

http://www.teachersdesk.org

Designed primarily for teachers in the upper elementary school grades, the focus of this site is reading, spelling, and writing.

Sites for Use in the Classroom with Children

Between the Lions

http://pbskids.org/lions/

Based on the popular PBS television show, this website features interactive stories, word play games, songs, and video clips.

Giggle Poetry

http://www.gigglepoetry.com

Featuring funny poetry for children, this website teaches children how to write different types of poems, allows kids to read and rate poetry, and offers tips for performing poetry plays.

NSTA Outstanding Science Trade Books for Students K-12

http://www.nsta.org/ostbc

The books that appear in these lists were selected as outstanding children's science trade books. They were selected by a book review panel appointed by the National Science Teachers Association (NSTA) and assembled in cooperation with the Children's Book Council (CBC). NSTA and CBC have cooperated on this bibliographic project since 1973.

Reading Is Fundamental

http://www.rif.org/readingplanet

Billed as "the nation's oldest and largest nonprofit children's literacy organization," RIF features a Game Station, Activity Lab, and Book Zone. The Daily Dose Reading Activity Calendar offers reading activity suggestions for every day of each month.

Reprinted with permission from Reading Is Fundamental.

The Story Place: The Children's Digital Library

http://www.storyplace.org

This educational site for children can be accessed in both English and Spanish. Kids will appreciate the animated stories complete with sound and extension activities.

Wacky Web Tales

http://www.eduplace.com/tales

Intended for grades 3 and above, this website allows students to write their own silly stories while learning about the parts of speech.

Winged Sandals

http://www.abc.net.au/arts/wingedsandals/default_lowband.htm

Children will enjoy this entertaining, multimedia site on Greek mythology. Hermes the messenger god leads users on an interactive exploration of gods, heroes, and mythical monsters.

Word Central

http://www.wordcentral.com

Powered by the Merriam-Webster Dictionary, this kid-friendly site features a Daily Buzzword (and archive), a Verse Composer, an encoder, and a Build-Your-Own Dictionary page.

Writing Den

http://www2.actden.com/writ_den

The Writing Den provides strategies and activities for students to improve their English language skills. Students can learn about constructing effective paragraphs, sentences, and essays in addition to signing up for a word of the day mailing list and exploring other subject areas.

 CHECK THEM OUT!

The Companion Website at **www.prenhall.com/cruz** has **Bonus Links** that are not included in the textbook!

CHAPTER 6

Mathematics Education

☞ REMEMBER!

Visit the Companion Website at **www.prenhall.com/cruz** for links to each website in this book.

As all elementary teachers know, mathematics education is more than just abstract concepts, formulas, and computations. Everyday life is permeated with challenges and opportunities to apply mathematical thinking and skills. The following professional organizations, journals, and standards play an essential role in mathematics education and the development of your teacher practices.

The National Council of Teachers of Mathematics (NCTM)

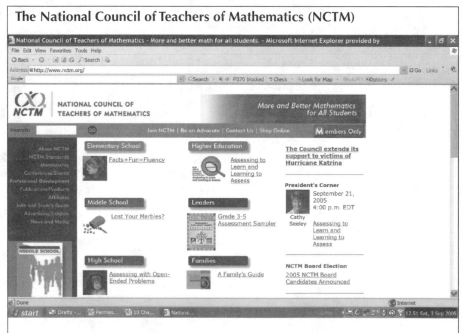

National Organizations and Standards on the Internet

Professional Organizations for Teachers of Mathematics

National Council of Teachers of Mathematics
http://www.nctm.org

Related Organizations

Mathematical Sciences Education Board
http://www7.nationalacademies.org/mseb/

The Mathematics Association of America
http://www.maa.org/

The Council for Technology in Mathematics Education
http://mathematicsforum.org/clime/

American Association for the Advancement of Science
http://www.aaas.org/

National Science Foundation
http://www.nsf.gov/

The National Academies of Science
http://www.nas.edu/

National and State Standards

NCTM provides an introduction to mathematics standards, **Principles and Standards for School Mathematics (PSSM)** at http://www.nctm.org/standards/introducing.htm and an interactive link at http://standards.nctm.org for the national standards.
The Annenberg/CPB at http://www.learner.org/theguide/ is a comprehensive guide to the mathematics and science education reform movement.
Your **state standards** can be found at http://edstandards.org/Standards.html or http://www.aligntoachieve.org/AchievePhaseII/basic-search.cfm.

ERIC and GEM

ERIC, http://www.eric.ed.gov/ (see Chapter 3), has almost 4,000 online articles; search for "mathematics education" AND "elementary education".

GEM, http://www.thegateway.org/browse (see Chapter 3), has over 9,000 possible lesson plans in mathematics education for use at the elementary school level.

Mathematics

Content Background Information

Math.com

http://www.math.com/teachers.html

Math.com includes a math library, lesson plans, and a teacher's center for topics ranging from basic math and geometry through calculus. Especially helpful are the downloadable "classroom resources" and "practice worksheets."

MathWorld

http://mathworld.wolfram.com/

This comprehensive website covers all the major subdivisions of mathematics and can be used for review and new learning. Perhaps most relevant to elementary school teachers are the sections on history and terminology and recreational mathematics, where there are explanations of mathematics in such things as checkers and chess.

PBS TeacherSource—Math

http://www.pbs.org/teachersource/math.htm

Funded by the federal government, this website has online videos of elementary school teachers demonstrating best practices and techniques in teaching math. Each is tied to a national standard. You should also use this site for other teaching fields.

Math Forum—Elementary Math Page

http://mathforum.org/sum95/math.forum/elem.html

Developed just for elementary school teachers, the Math Forum is a gateway site with a wealth of classroom materials and Internet links. By going to the Classroom Materials section, users can access lesson plans, online glossaries, and mathematical puzzles appropriate for elementary-aged children.

Ask Dr. Math

http://mathforum.org/library/drmath/drmath.elem.html

Sponsored by Drexel University, Dr. Math is part of the **Math Forum** website. It has an extensive elementary section that includes content organized by topics based on questions posed by students and answers given by math experts. Users can access word problems, worksheets, puzzles, and links to other resources on the Internet. In addition, it has a teacher's lounge where teachers share ideas and answer questions posed by other teachers.

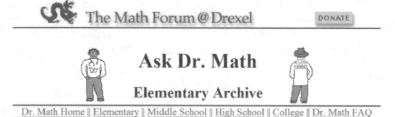

Reprinted with permission from the Math Forum @ Drexel.

Math Archives

http://archives.math.utk.edu/topics/

This site has a large collection of links to other sites categorized by grade level for arithmetic and geometry as well as a collection of downloadable software for student use and lesson plans. Users can find specific information quickly by using the site's search engine or by browsing categories such as Applied Mathematics, Statistics, or Art & Music.

The MacTutor History of Mathematics archive

http://www-groups.dcs.st-and.ac.uk/~history/index.html

This site contains a history of mathematics, biographies of mathematicians, and timelines. A changing "Mathematicians of the Day" features mathematicians who were born or died on each day of the year and provides a downloadable, illustrated poster for many of them.

Multimedia Math Glossary

http://www.hbschool.com/glossary/math2/ index3.html

A product of Harcourt publishers, this website has a listing by grade level of the grade-appropriate terms children should know about mathematics. By selecting a grade level and then clicking on a term, there is a simulation appropriate for children of the concept and by clicking on the speaker icon, the word is stated. This site can be used with children in the classroom in a whole-class setting or at PC work stations.

Mathematics & Children's Literature

http://sci.tamucc.edu/%7Eeyoung /literature.html

This site has a neatly organized listing of children's books, grade level, and topic with a live link that takes you to the Amazon.com page for the book. Mathematical topics such as fractions, geometry, and money each have suggested stories and teaching ideas.

The Math League

http://www.mathleague.com/

The Math League supports math competitions starting in fourth grade. Samples of problems are provided as well as a handy reference guide for math topics for grades 4 through 8, complete with examples, definitions, and explanations.

The Geometry Junkyard

http://www.ics.uci.edu/~eppstein/junkyard/

Geometry in Action

http://www.ics.uci.edu/~eppstein/geom.html

These websites are hosted by a University of California professor and have everything on geometry from lecture notes, research excerpts, papers, abstracts, programs, and problems.

StudyWorks Online

http://www.studyworksonline.com/ cda/explorations/main/0,,NAV2-21,00.html

This site has a geometry page that lists common problems, such as congruent angles, along with an interactive feature that walks the viewer through the solution using easy-to-understand explanations and visuals.

Lesson Plans, Strategies, and Materials

NCTM Reflections

http://my.nctm.org/eresources/reflections/index.htm

NCTM's Reflections contains videos of teachers delivering mathematics lessons that allow teachers to reflect on their approach to teaching mathematics.

Learner.org

http://www.learner.org/resources/browse.html?discipline=5&grade=2&imageField2.
    x=10&imageField2.y=21

This site offers a series of streaming videos on math assessment techniques that teachers can use to ensure that their students are succeeding.

Illuminations

http://illuminations.nctm.org/index.aspx

Sponsored by NCTM, this site offers detailed and model lesson plans by grade level, each tied to the national standards.

Eisenhower National Clearinghouse

http://www.goenc.com/

This federal initiative to improve mathematics and science has over 20,000 resources that can be selected through a search engine by grade level and type. However, there is a school or district fee for full access.

PBS: TeacherSource—Math

http://www.pbs.org/teachersource/math.htm

At PBS, you can select grade-level-appropriate lesson plans based on different subjects, consider reviews of children's books, and go to links to other mathematics lesson plans sites. Several of the lesson plans correlate with a PBS show, promoting a multimedia approach in teaching.

About Mathematics

http://math.about.com/od/arithmetic/

This website has lesson plans, games in the Recreational Math section, worksheets, and links to other websites with additional resources. Teachers and students can download flash cards, a glossary, and entertaining math tricks.

Smile

http://www.iit.edu/~smile/

The Science and Mathematics Initiative for Learning Enhancement (SMILE) website includes a large number of concise lesson plans organized by topics such as geometry and measurement, patterns and logic, probability, and practical math.

Figure This!

http://www.figurethis.org

In this site, go to the Math Index and select one of the challenges for categories such as geometry or measurement to view how the problems are structured. What makes this site unique is

that the *Figure This!* challenges are an easy and enjoyable way to get parents involved with their child's mathematics education (see PowerPoint presentation under Teacher Corner).

AAA Math (All About Math)

http://www.aaamath.com/

This site is organized by grade level and topic (ordering numbers, rations, etc.) or by topic, and for each there is a definition, example, and hundreds of pages of practice opportunities.

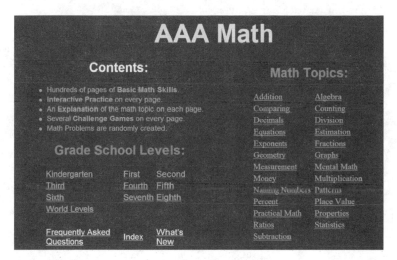

Reprinted with permission.

edHelper.com—Math

http://www.edhelper.com/math.htm

edHelper.com's math section restricts options (such as answer keys to worksheets) to members. But, as an example, select Grade 2 Math, scroll down to Ordering Numbers, and select Ordering Mixed Review. A new window will open and you can print the worksheet for use in your classroom.

Montessori Math Album

http://www.ux1.eiu.edu/~cfsjy/mts/math/_link.htm

The application of Montessori method to mathematics is demonstrated through almost 50 lesson plans. The lessons are designed for lower elementary or pre-kindergarten. Although most of them are dependent on Montessori manipulative materials, many can be modified for regular classroom use.

Math Forum: Teacher2Teacher

http://www.mathforum.com/t2t/discuss/

At Teacher2Teacher, a bulletin board discussion is housed in the Teacher's Lounge. There are hundreds of discussion topics related to content and methods that you can use to gain valuable insights into mathematics education at the elementary school level.

SCORE Mathematics Lessons

http://score.kings.k12.ca.us/lessons.html

These lessons were written by teachers in California and are useful for teachers in the others states as well. The Lessons for K-7 feature plans for topics such as Number Sense, Algebra and Functions, and Mathematical Reasoning.

Sites for use in the Classroom with Children

National Library of Virtual Manipulatives

http://nlvm.usu.edu/en/nav /vlibrary.html

These online manipulatives are grouped by grade-level ranges and topic and can be used in whole-class instruction or at PC stations. The index is broken down by categories such as Number and Operations, Geometry, and Measurement.

Mathematics Resource Site

http://www.carrollk12.org/instruction/elemcurric/math/teacher.htm

Developed by a school district, this site has extensive and practical resources of all kinds for elementary mathematics teachers. There are various graphic organizers, worksheets, and reference tables at the Basic Facts section and downloadable PowerPoint presentations at PP Presentations.

Songs for Teaching

http://www.songsforteaching.com/mathsongs.htm

Who would have thought that there are over 75 songs that can be used to teach mathematics? When you click on a song, a new page will open and you can choose to hear the song with a program such as Windows Media; the lyrics are provided for you to use in class.

Reprinted with permission from Songs for Teaching.

mathDrill

http://www.mathdrill.com/

This site would be best used with students at PC stations. There are 86 levels of difficulty that can be use to select problems in multiple categories. Students receive immediate feedback while they practice their mathematics.

A+Math

http://www.aplusmath.com/Flashcards/

With A+Math you can create custom flash cards and worksheets. In addition there are online games that can be used as whole-class activities.

Cool Math

http://www.coolmath.com

This fully interactive site allows the children to sharpen basic math skills, play math-related games, and explore new math concepts.

Math Advantage

http://www.hbschool.com/menus/L_math.html

Harcourt Brace's Learning Site has clickable, interactive links that are based on their textbook series that are available to all teachers. As an example, select Grade and then Chapter 10. The pattern builder uses a keyboard with live notes to demonstrate the concept of a pattern.

KidsNumbers.com

http://www.kidsnumbers.com/

This is an interactive website where children can test their addition, subtraction, multiplication, and division skills with interactive flash cards and games.

ReviseWise Maths

http://www.bbc.co.uk/schools/revisewise/maths/

The site of the British Broadcasting Company organizes a lesson around an activity, fact sheet, worksheet, and test for use with students in a number of elementary mathematics topics.

Dositey.com

http://www.dositey.com/homek2.htm

This site has interactive, multimedia games and problem-solving activities that can be used in whole-class settings or with students in groups.

The ArithmAttack

http://www.saab.org/mathdrills/attack.html

Students can "attack" math problems and set a timer to determine how well they do with adding, subtracting, dividing, and multiplying.

The ArithmAttack

CHECK THEM OUT!
The Companion Website at **www.prenhall.com/cruz** has **Bonus Links** that are not included in the textbook!

CHAPTER 7

Science and Technology Education

The Internet makes possible the teaching of science and technology more dynamic, more accurate, and more engaging than ever before. The following professional organizations, journals, and standards play an essential role in science education and the development of your teacher practices.

The National Science Teachers Association (NSTA)

Included with permission from the National Science Teachers Association copyright © 2005.

National Organizations and Standards on the Internet

Professional Organizations for Teachers of Science

National Science Teachers Association
http://www.nsta.org/

National Academy of Sciences
http://www.nas.edu/

American Association for the Advancement of Science
http://www.aaas.org/

Eisenhower National Clearinghouse
http://www.enc.org/

National Science Foundation
http://www.nsf.gov/

National Association for Research in Science Teaching
http://www2.educ.sfu.ca/narstsite/

National Middle Level Science Teachers Association
http://www.nmlsta.org/

Related Organizations

American Association of Physics Teachers
http://www.aapt.org/

National Association of Biology Teachers
http://www.nabt.org/

The American Chemistry Society
http://www.chemistry.org/portal/a/c/s/1/ home.html

Chemical Heritage Foundation
http://www.chemheritage.org/

American Institute of Physics
http://www.aip.org/

American Society of Plant Biologists
http://www.aspb.org/

National Association of Geoscience Teachers
http://www.nagt.org/

National Earth Science Teachers Association
http://www.nesta.org/

The Geological Society of America
http://www.geosociety.org/educate

History of Science Society
http://www.hssonline.org/

National and State Standards

Project 2061 Benchmarks
http://www.project2061.org/tools/benchol/bolintro.htm

Continued

The National Science Education Standards
http://stills.nap.edu/html/nses/

INTASC Standards for Science Teacher Education
http://www.ccsso.org/content/ pdfs/ScienceStandards.pdf

Your state standards **can be found** at
http://edstandards.org/Standards.html or
http://www.aligntoachieve.org/AchievePhaseII/basic-search.cfm.

ERIC and GEM

ERIC, http://www.eric.ed.gov/ (see Chapter 3), has almost 2,000 online articles; search for "science education" AND "elementary education".

GEM, http://www.thegateway.org/browse (see Chapter 3), has over 25,000 possible lesson plans in science for use at the elementary school level.

For this chapter, the websites are organized under the headings of Earth and Space Sciences, Life Sciences, and Physical Sciences and Technology. However, many of the sites, although placed in one of these categories, will have resources that can be used in all three subject areas.

Earth and Space Sciences

Content Background Information

The Sourcebook for Teaching Science

http://www.csun.edu/~vceed002/chapters/thinking/index.html

This is a gateway to information on teaching science that includes chapters on thinking scientifically, problem solving, and communicating science concepts with examples, lesson plans, and activities that cover the range of science.

Eric Weisstein's World of Scientific Biography

http://scienceworld.wolfram.com/biography/

Organized by branch of science, chronologically, and by name, this award-winning site provides a brief biography of each major scientist with a picture when available.

Exploring the Environment

http://www.cotf.edu/ete/teacher/introduction.html

Although designed for high school students, Exploring the Environment™ (ETE) is a series of interdisciplinary, problem-based learning (PBL) modules that can help elementary school teachers better understand environmental issues.

Astronomy.com

http://www.astronomy.com/asy/default.aspx

An excellent starting point to brush up on your knowledge of space. This site has an introduction to astronomy as well as a number of images appropriate for use in class.

PhysLink.com

http://www.physlink.com/Education/Astronomy.cfm

PhysLink.com is a comprehensive astronomy and physics online education, research, and reference website that can provide valuable background resources.

National Aeronautics and Space Administration

http://www.nasa.gov/home/ index.html?skipIntro=1

NASA has developed a large amount of information on space, meteorology, and earth science in general. From its site, you can click on For Kids, For Students, and For Educators; the two sections that provide rich resources for teachers under educators are Classroom Subjects and Educational Materials.

Geology.com

http://geology.com/

A dictionary of geology terms is provided along with sections on Paleontology, Minerals and Rocks, Maps and Satellite Images (including a map and explanation of the geology of each state), Earthquakes, Floods, and other related topics.

Meteorology A to Z

http://www.wxdude.com/topics.html

Covers over 50 key terms in meteorology by providing a clickable link to a resource with detailed information. Site also has a hip-hop song with links about weather.

Newton's Apple

http://www.tpt.org/newtons/alpha.html

The popular science TV show has posted Discussions based on its TV series. Topics such as acid rain, bee stings, baseball bats—and hundreds of others—are included.

NESTAnet

http://www.nestanet.org/

The National Earth Science Teachers Association has links to such topics as Earth History through Oceanography and special links under Earth News on current events with hurricanes and tornadoes as well as detailing explanations of each.

The Great Idea Finder

http://www.ideafinder.com/history/of_inventions.htm

Listed from A to Z, this site has both the myths about inventions and their accurate history and origin.

Lesson Plans, Strategies, and Materials

The Franklin Institute

http://sln.fi.edu/learn.html

The Franklin Institute is a science museum and offers online exhibits that can be used in class and by teachers. It offers lesson plans on numerous science topics under Community Science Action Guides and Educators Keystone Science Network. The online exhibit on the human heart is particularly well done.

Windows to the Universe

http://www.windows.ucar.edu/windows.html

This engaging site has an impressive list of lesson plans and activities for earth and space science and can also be used in the classroom with students.

Smithsonian's Ocean Planet

http://seawifs.gsfc.nasa.gov/OCEAN_PLANET/ HTML/search_educational_materials.html

A large number of educational materials based on the Ocean Planet Exhibition at the Smithsonian.

Newton's Apple

http://www.tpt.org/newtons/alpha.html

The popular science TV show has posted Discussions based on its TV series on topics such as acid rain, bee stings, and so on. The discussion provides the background information.

Amazing Space

http://amazing-space.stsci.edu/eds/

Amazing Space combines a section on astronomy basics with a teacher's tools section with materials and overviews, including instructions and suggestions for using the resources.

Digital Library for Earth System Education

http://www.dlese.org/dds/index.jsp

Sponsored by NSF, under educational resources, you will find over 6,000 lesson plans or materials for elementary education instruction in all facets of earth science education.

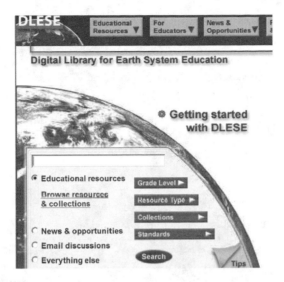

Reprinted with permission from the Digital Library for Earth System Education.

Exploring Planets in the Classroom Hands-on Activities

http://www.space grant.hawaii.edu/class_acts/

This site has over 25 hands-on science activities for the classroom with materials and directions for the teacher.

National Weather Service

http://www.nws.noaa.gov/

There are hundreds of images and depictions of the United States having to do with weather forecasts, water quality, natural hazards, and the like. Students will like accessing their local information.

The Weather Unit

http://faldo.atmos.uiuc.edu/w_unit/weather.html

The weather unit is a thematic lesson plan integrating math, social studies, sciences, music, arts, and so on.

U.S. Environmental Protection Agency

http://www.epa.gov/safewater/ kids/kids_k-3.html

The EPA has lesson plans and materials for teachers and games and activities for students organized by lower and upper elementary grade levels.

Colorful Landform Atlas of the United States

http://fermi.jhuapl.edu/states/states.html

This site has hundreds of four-color images organized by each state based on weather and landform patterns.

Sites for Use in the Classroom with Children

Astronomy for Kids

http://www.dustbunny.com/afk/

This site has several sections. The sections are not long and all of them should be easily understood by kids of all ages.

Earth and Moon Viewer

http://www.fourmilab.ch/earthview/vplanet.html

This interactive site allows you to view earth in various forms, such as based on longitude and latitude and different satellites.

NASA for Kids

http://www.nasa.gov/audience/forkids/home/index.html

NASA has created a website with games, stories, and activities for children.

KidsAstronomy.com

http://www.kidsastronomy.com/solar_system.htm

This children's website about the solar system is easily navigable and written with children in mind.

Scientific American.com—Ask the Experts

http://www.sciam.com/askexpert_directory.cfm

At *Scientific American*, you can ask an expert any question you may have about a science topic.

Life Sciences

Content Background Information

The Biology Place

http://www.phschool.com/science/biology_place/index.html

Offered by Pearson Publishing, this site provides online explanations, activities, and laboratory exercises that will allow you to brush up on your biology and download materials for your classroom.

Human Biology

http://www.people.virginia.edu/~rjh9u/humbiol993.html

The materials are from a college course in human biology. What makes the site particularly useful to elementary school teachers is that the topics are used to explain the biology of such popular topics as cloning, hormones, and immune systems.

Marine Biology Web

http://life.bio.sunysb.edu/marinebio/mbweb.html

Marine biology links listed at the website include pictures of organisms, information on habitats by geographic locations, marine life, and a glossary of marine biology terms.

NABT Resource Links

http://www.nabt.org/sub/links_generalbio.asp

The National Association of Biology Teachers has a comprehensive set of links by topic that provides resources that are adaptable to the elementary classroom.

Genetics: Children Resemble Their Parents

http://www.dnaftb.org/dnaftb/1/concept/

This site can be used to explain genetics using the theme of children and how they resemble their parents. The site has both background content information for teachers and animations for children.

Endangered Species Themes Page

http://www.cln.org/themes/endangered.html

This page has links to lesson plans and background content information on endangered species.

Botany.com Encyclopedia of Plants

http://www.botany.com/

This encyclopedia has descriptions of plant life with both their common and Latin names.

Lesson Plans, Strategies, and Materials

Biology Lesson Plans for Elementary School Teachers

http://www.biology lessons.sdsu.edu/about/index.html

This site provides detailed lesson plans on molecules and cells and organism development that can be downloaded. The lesson plans include graphs, diagrams, and other visual features.

Southwest Educational Development Laboratory Interdisciplinary Lesson Plans

http://www.sedl.org/scimath/pasopartners/

This site includes math and science lesson plans in English and Spanish that are appropriate for lower elementary grades.

Discovery School.com—Human Body

http://school.discovery.com/lessonplans/body.html

Although this site lists only four lesson plans for grades 1 through 4, the other lesson plans could be modified for the elementary school classroom.

eNature

http://www.enature.com/home/

Sponsored by the National Wildlife Federation, this site has over 5,000 types of wildlife with pictures, descriptions, and information that can be sorted by various categories, types, and locations.

American Society of Plant Biologists—K-12 Resources

http://www.aspb.org/ education/NEWK12.CFM

The American Society of Plant Biologists has an extensive listing of lessons, activities, and materials for the elementary classroom.

American Museum of Natural History

http://amnh.org/education/resources/ rfl.php?set=b&intro=true

The site has a large number of lesson plans organized into categories including biology, paleontology, astronomy, earth science, and anthropology.

Education Planet

http://www.educationplanet.com/search/Science

This multipurpose site for lesson plans and materials has subcategories that allow teachers to zero in on topics. As an example, it has over 2,000 lesson plans on animals and 1,800 website links that you can access from the home page, selecting Science, and then Animals. This site should be used for all subjects.

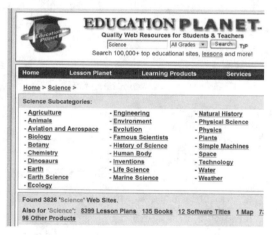

Reprinted with permission from Education Planet.

Neuroscience for Kids

http://faculty.washington.edu/chudler/introb.html

This site not only provides the teacher the background knowledge for an investigation of the neurological systems, but also provides an extraordinary number of depictions and examples, lesson plans, and experiments.

Scott's Botanical Links

http://www.ou.edu/cas/botany-micro/bot-linx/subject/

A comprehensive listing of annotated links to multimedia, images, lesson plans, and activities related to plant life.

Sites for Use in the Classroom with Children

Cells Alive!

http://www.cellsalive.com/

This site includes multiple interactive, downloadable video clips and still images of various cells and living organisms with a particularly useful explanation of the role they play in life cycles.

Kids Do Ecology

http://www.nceas.ucsb.edu/nceas-web/kids/

Children can learn about ecology by paging through images and definitions about biomes and marine mammals.

Rader's Biology4Kids, Chemistry4Kids, and Geography4Kids

http://www. biology4kids.com/

http://www.chem4kids.com/

http://www.geography4kids.com/

These sites explain biology, chemistry, and geography in a way that is appropriate for elementary school-aged students. It is also an excellent resource for whole class instruction and materials.

Bucket Buddies

http://www.k12science.org/curriculum/bucketproj/index.html

Students around the United States and other countries collect samples from local ponds to answer questions such as "Are the organisms found in pond water the same all over the world?"

Reprinted with permission of CIESE.

EstuaryLIVE

http://www.estuarylive.org/

Live, on-demand video of over 20 estuaries is available to be shown to whole class or to students at PC stations.

The Yuckiest Site on the Internet

http://yucky.kids.discovery.com/flash/body/

A very creative site that presents information to students in a witty format. The site includes interactive explanations to such questions as why humans get gas, games, and other things kids find yucky such as worms and roaches.

Virtual Frog Dissection Kit

http://froggy.lbl.gov/virtual

At this site, you can dissect a frog online.

Click on the frog to dive  into the kit.

Physical Sciences and Technology

Content Background Information

Physics 2000

http://www.colorado.edu/physics/2000/index.pl

By clicking on each physics topic in the table of contents, the topics are explained using a question-and-answer approach that is easy to understand.

Chemistry Resources

http://people.clarkson.edu/~rosen2/webwork.htm

This site is a neatly organized listing of information on chemistry that can provide background information or review.

Famous Inventions: A to Z

http://inventors.about.com/library/bl/bl12.htm

About.com offers a timeline and history of major inventions that shaped the world.

A Century of Physics

http://timeline.aps.org/APS/

This interactive timeline shows the major advancements in technology, physics, biology, astronomy, and chemistry depicted with explanations.

Physics for Beginners

http://physics.webplasma.com/physicstoc.html

The information is a primer for teachers who know very little about physics.

Lesson Plans, Strategies, and Materials

Elementary School Lesson Plans

http://www.physics.rutgers.edu/hex/visit/lesson/lesson_links1.html

This site has hundreds of lesson plans listed by topics such as force and motion, properties of matter, magnetism, and energy. Each lesson plan has an understandable title and grade level to help you choose, and the plans are easy to read and follow.

Physical Sciences Resource Center

http://www.compadre.org/psrc/search/browse.cfm?browse=gs

Lesson plans, experiments, simulations, and learner activities are catalogued for each selection for elementary (and check out middle school) education teachers.

Physical Science Activity Manual

http://www.utm.edu/departments/cece/cesme/PSAM/PSAM.shtml

The Physical Science Activity Manual contains 34 hands-on activities to bring excitement to your classroom.

TryScience

http://www.tryscience.org/experiments/experiments_home.html

TryScience lists almost 90 experiments from all branches of science with an online interactive option for whole-class instruction or an offline option that provides the teacher with the background information to conduct the experiment.

BOCES Science Activities

http://www.monroe2boces.org/programs.cfm?sublevel=350&subsubpage=82&subpage=54&master=3

Grouped into fall, winter, spring, and summer science activities, this site has over 100 science lessons from the structure of a raindrop to the five senses in the spring.

Sites for Use in the Classroom with Children

Thinking Fountain

http://www.smm.org/sln/tf/nav/tfatoz.html

The Thinking Fountain is an interactive website from the Science Museum of Minnesota, and its A to Z listing of course materials includes activities and children's books.

A to Z

A to Z is an alphabetical list of the Thinking Fountain.
Thinking Fountain is always changing and growing! You'll find:
- Activities and ideas
- Galleries to show your work
- Books you can use
- Surprises inspired by Thinking Fountain

A B C D E F G H I J K L M N O P Q R S T U V W X Y Z

Reprinted with permission.

Science Toys

http://scitoys.com/

Teachers can make "toys" with common household materials, often in only a few minutes, that demonstrate fascinating scientific principles such as magnetism, rocket engine, or battery.

The History of Invention

http://www.cbc.ca/kids/general/the-lab/history-of-invention/default.html

This interactive timeline can be used by students in a whole-class lesson or at PC stations.

The Atoms Family

http://www.miamisci.org/af/sln/

This resource, from the Miami Museum of Science, contains educational activities relating to different forms of energy, and are presented by famous gothic horror characters.

Sci4Kids

http://www.ars.usda.gov/is/kids

This is an interactive, engaging website that children can navigate to learn about science through stories about animals, rain, and so on.

 CHECK THEM OUT!

The Companion Website at **www.prenhall.com/cruz** has **Bonus Links** that are not included in the textbook!

CHAPTER 8

Social Studies

☞ **REMEMBER!**
Visit the Companion Website at **www.prenhall.com/cruz** for links to each website in this book.

The cliché about the world seeming to get smaller does seem to be true when educators use the Internet to enhance social studies instruction. Students and teachers now have access to information, cultures, and real-time current events that can make social studies come alive as never before. The following professional organizations and standards play an essential role in social studies education and the development of your teacher practices.

The National Council for the Social Studies (NCSS)

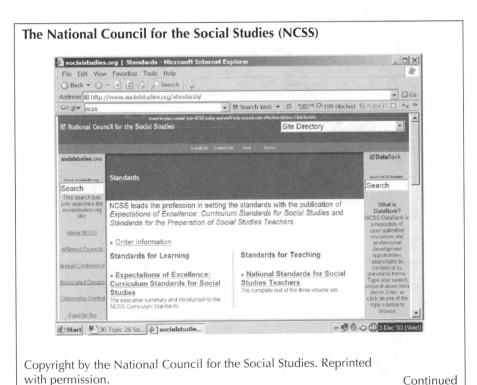

Copyright by the National Council for the Social Studies. Reprinted with permission.

Continued

National Organizations and Standards on the Internet

Professional Organizations for Teachers of Social Studies

National Council for the Social Studies (NCSS)
http://www.ncss.org/ or www.socialstudies.org

Related Organizations

National Center for History in the Schools
http://www.sscnet.ucla.edu/nchs/

Organization of American Historians
http://www.oah.org/

American Historical Association
http://www.theaha.org/

National Council for History Education
http://www.history.org/nche

American Studies Association
http://www.georgetown.edu/crossroads/assainfo.html

National Center on Education and the Economy
http://www.ncee.org

National Association of Economic Educators
http://ecedweb.unomaha.edu/naee/naeepamp.htm

The National Council for Geographic Education
http://www.ncge.org

Association of American Geographers
http://www.aag.org/intro.html

The American Geographical Society
http://www.amergeog.org/index.html

The Center for Civic Education
http://www.civiced.org/index.html

The American Political Science Association
http://www.apsanet.org/

American Anthropological Association
http://www.aaanet.org

American Psychological Association
http://www.apa.org

American Sociological Association
http://www.asanet.org

National and State Standards

Expectations of Excellence: Curriculum Standards for Social Studies
http://www.socialstudies.org/standards/

National Standards for History
http://www.sscnet.ucla.edu/nchs/standards/thinkingk-4.html

National Content Standards in Economics
http://www.economicsamerica.org/standards/contents.html

National Geography Standards

http://www.ncge.org/publications/tutorial/standards/

National Standards for Civics and Government

http://www.civiced.org/curriculum.html

INTASC Standards for Social Studies Teacher Education are in development, see http://www.ccsso.org/.

Your **state standards** can be found at http://edstandards.org/Standards.html or http://www.aligntoachieve.org/AchievePhaseII/basic-search.cfm.

ERIC, GEM, and Blue Web'N

ERIC, http://www.eric.ed.gov/ (see Chapter 3), has almost 3,100 online articles; search for "social studies" AND "elementary education".

GEM, http://www.thegateway.org/browse (see Chapter 3), has over 10,000 possible lesson plans in social studies for use at the elementary school level.

The Knowledge Network Explorer at http://www.kn.pacbell.com/wired/bluewebn/ contentarea.cfm?cid=8 links to almost 1,000 other sites on a broad range of social studies disciplines and can be searched by grade level.

U.S. History

Content Background Information

National Endowment for the Humanities

http://edsitement.neh.gov/

The EDSITEment website includes website links and lesson plans by grade level for not only history and social studies, but also art and culture, literature and language arts, and foreign language.

National Women's History Museum

http://www.nwhm.org

The history of the American suffragist movement is the focus of this website, although other topics related to women's history are covered as well. Features include a timeline of major events in women's rights, a cyber museum, an image gallery, and an interactive quiz. A link to Additional Resources provides a bibliography of useful books and other online resources.

National Park Service: Links to the Past

http://www.cr.nps.gov/colherit.htm

The NPS's website provides links to the people, places, objects, and events of our nation's past. Treasures of the Nation offers images and descriptions of hundreds of items in the

NPS | Links to the Past

Explore . . .

People, Places, Objects and Events

museum collections. Over 100 lesson plans are available in Teaching with Historic Places, and National Park Service historians are available to field online queries.

The Star-Spangled Banner

http://www.americanhistory.si.edu/ssb

This Smithsonian Institution website offers detailed information about Old Glory, preservation efforts, and a Test Your Knowledge site. Teachers will find the educator's page especially helpful, with a K-8 teacher's manual, a bibliography, and ideas for using the site with children.

World Wide Web—Virtual Library: U.S. History

http://vlib.iue.it/history/USA/

This portal site provides thousands of links to U.S. history resources. Maps, timelines, research articles, and background readings are just some of the categories offered under detailed topics broken down by historical eras and events.

Lesson Plans, Strategies, and Materials

The History Place

http://www.historyplace.com/

This website offers historical photos, speeches, and other primary source documents that can bring immediacy to the classroom. A gallery of presidential portraits also includes the sounds of the presidents from FDR to President Bush. The Personal Histories section offers diaries and first-person accounts of historical events, many from the perspective of a child.

The Library of Congress: American Memory

http://memory.loc.gov/ammem

This considerable collection of U.S. treasures can be browsed by topics such as African American History, Native American History, Presidents, and Sports. In addition to digitized print

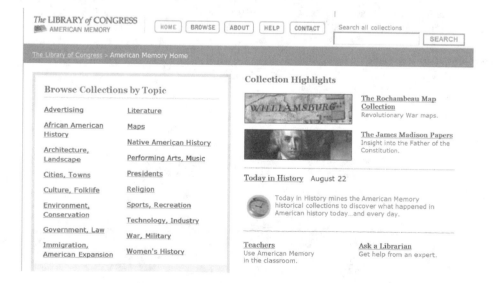

materials, the historical collections also offer resources in both audio and visual formats. The Learning Page, a special link for teachers (http://memory.loc.gov/learn), provides lesson plans, interactive puzzles and games, and ideas for collaborative projects.

The National Archives and Records Administration

http://www.archives.gov/digital_classroom/

The Digital Classroom Web page of the NARA has primary source documents, worksheets for analysis, and images for use in the classroom. The Teaching with Documents section is replete with lesson plans and teaching ideas. The searchable engine allows you to find specific documents easily. A related site (http://www.ourdocuments.gov) provides electronic versions of 100 milestone documents in our nation's history.

Core Knowledge

http://www.coreknowledge.org/CK/resrcs/lessons/index.htm

The Core Knowledge website has an extensive set of lesson plans and materials for use in American history and government as well as world history. Many of the lessons are interdisciplinary.

Sites for Use in the Classroom with Children

America Dreams . . . through the Decades

http://memory.loc.gov/ammem/ndlpedu/lessons/97/dream/

This Library of Congress WebQuest allows students to explore U.S. history through each of the decades of the 21st century. Working in teams, students take on the personas of a photographer, lawyer, poet, politician, producer, comedian, musician, and newspaper reporter. The task and all roles are thoroughly explained. The teacher section lays out all curriculum standards, implementation strategies, and tools for assessment.

Songs for Teaching—Social Studies

http://www.songsforteaching.com/socialstudiessongs.htm

Music has long been recognized as an effective tool for teaching young children. This website provides lyrics—and in many cases audio files—for a large variety of songs that can be used in the classroom.

HistoryWired: A Few of Our Favorite Things

http://historywired.si.edu

This experimental program sponsored by the Smithsonian Institution allows visitors to take a virtual tour of selected objects (most not currently on exhibit) from the vast collections of the National Museum of American History. By moving your mouse over the various categories (e.g., Home, Clothing, Transportation, Sports) students can first see a thumbnail image of the object to aid in selection. Once an object is selected, a description is provided along with relevant quotes, notes, and links to related objects.

Smithsonian Institution: History and Culture

http://www.si.edu/history_and_culture

Our American heritage can be explored in a number of ways through the Smithsonian's famous collection. The site is user friendly, and when students navigate it they will find entries and artifacts on subjects as diverse as our nation's presidents, *Brown* v. *The Board of Education*, Lewis and Clark, and Julia Child's kitchen.

World History

Content Background Information

EyeWitness to History

http://www.eyewitnesstohistory.com

This rather irreverent website is billed as "history through the eyes of those who lived it." It includes highly descriptive eyewitness accounts, photos, and audio clips.

The History Channel

http://www.historychannel.com

Linked to the cable channel, this site offers a wealth of articles, biographies, historic speeches, and video clips. The Classroom Link provides teachers with a free newsletter, study guides, quizzes, and teaching ideas. A special feature is This Day in History, which allows you each day to post important events in your classroom and for kids to find out what happened on their birthday.

Histor eSearch and World Wide Web—Virtual Library: World History

http://www.snowcrest.net/jmike and http://vlib.iue.it/history/index.html

These comprehensive sites feature hundreds of links to sites related to modern and ancient world history, Asian history, Latin American history, and African history, among others. A link to historical documents provides dozens of original letters, patent applications, executive orders, and the like, and you can gather information by country, period, and so on.

Mr.Dowling.com

http://www.mrdowling.com

Topics on this teacher-friendly site range from pre-history to contemporary regions and conflicts. Clicking on each topic gives you a thumbnail sketch and historical timeline. There are also hundreds of free lesson plans, study guides, homework assignments, and exams. A helpful feature is that users can edit the lesson plans online before printing.

Lesson Plans, Strategies, and Materials

Awesome Library: K-12 Social Studies Lesson Plans

http://www.awesomelibrary.org/social.html

General social studies topics such as history, economics, and government are enhanced by the inclusion of multicultural activities, multidisciplinary lessons, and information related to holidays. Lists are further broken down by categories such as lesson plans, materials, and projects.

Kathy Schrock's Guide for Educators: History and Social Studies

http://school.discovery.com/schrockguide/history/histg.html

This gateway site is maintained daily for accuracy and breadth. An exhaustive array of social studies topics are offered with links to lesson plans, timelines, calendars, cartoons, discussions, and images.

Mr. Donn's World History Page

http://members.aol.com/MrDonnHistory/World.html

This award-winning site covers world history from medieval times through the 21st century. Lesson plans, learning activities, and worksheets are provided in addition to links to timelines, world holidays, and other online services and resources related to world history.

Sites for Use in the Classroom with Children

BBC Modern World History

http://www.bbc.co.uk/history

With topics ranging from Ancient History to World War II, this site maintained by the British Broadcasting Corporation has a variety of features for both students and teachers. The interactive animations, including animated maps, games, and timelines, require Shockwave software (which is available on the site). The History for Kids link offers images, sounds, and cartoons appropriate for the elementary grades.

Tales of Wonder

http://www.darsie.net/talesofwonder

Students can access this award-winning collection of folk and fairy tales by clicking on a region of the world. Virtually all countries of the world are represented. Most appropriate for upper elementary grade readers, the stories are reflective of each culture's unique characteristics and heritage while underscoring humanity's common heritage of storytelling.

Geography

Content Background Information

The CIA World Factbook

http://www.cia.gov/cia/publications/factbook/index.html

For the world's most current and accurate information, teachers should turn to the CIA's *World Factbook*. Every nation in the world is represented with current maps, country profiles, flags of the world, and coverage of global issues.

50states.com

http://www.50states.com/

For quick, easy-to-access information on the 50 states in the union, this site is easily navigated. In addition to statistical, geographical, and historical information, state symbols, flags, and songs are included. For the latter, sheet music and lyrics are provided, and the melodies can be heard with Real Player software.

National Atlas of the United States

http://www.nationalatlas.gov

This dynamic site provides educators with informative articles on a variety of topics (e.g., climate, people, and transportation). Developed by the U.S. Geological Survey, this online atlas of the United States features both natural and social-cultural landscapes. Interactive maps provide unusual illustrations of natural phenomena. Teachers wanting to create and customize maps will find this site extremely useful.

Lesson Plans, Strategies, and Materials

Atlapedia Online

http://www.atlapedia.com

Full-color maps, key facts, and statistical data on all countries of the world can be accessed on this site. Information about climate, population, history, culture, religion, and language is accurate and straightforward. Teachers can search for information by country name or browse the world map section.

Atlapedia Online contains full color physical maps, political maps as well as key facts and statistics on countries of the world.

Reprinted with permission from Atlapedia Online.

Earth from Space

http://earth.jsc.nasa.gov/sseop/efs

Using images acquired by astronauts, this NASA website offers high-resolution images of Earth as viewed from space. Images include cities and geographic regions, Earth-human interactions, and hurricanes and weather.

The GLOBE Program

http://www.globe.gov/fsl/welcome.html

The GLOBE Program's Teachers Guide is available for online viewing, printing, or downloading. Each chapter and the individual protocols, learning activities, data sheets, and field guides are available in PDF format. Lessons can be searched by both concept and grade level. The Resource Room offers links to a myriad of other useful sites. Interactive activities for students are also provided.

The National Council for Geographic Education

http://www.ncge.org

The Geography Club is a feature of the National Council for Geographic Education especially for elementary school teachers. In addition to a free downloadable PowerPoint presentation, educators can access three month's worth of activities and student worksheets.

National Geographic Xpeditions

http://www.nationalgeographic.com/xpeditions

This comprehensive site features lesson plans, activities, images, and maps that are all tied to the 18 U.S. National Geography Standards. Particularly helpful for teachers is that the lesson plans are broken down by grade level range (e.g., K–2, 3–5). Also be sure to check out One-Stop Research (http://www.nationalgeographic.com/onestop), National Geographic's research Web page providing a search engine for the entire site.

World Wise Schools

http://www.peacecorps.gov/wws/educators

A kind of pen pal system, this site operated by the Peace Corps seeks to promote global awareness. The teacher-tested lesson plans and resources are organized by topic, geographic area, and grade level. A useful Country Information section provides accurate statistics and information on countries throughout the world.

Sites for Use in the Classroom with Children

National Geographic for Kids

http://www.nationalgeographic.com/kids

This high-quality site sponsored by National Geographic is the premier geography website for children. Features include stories, games, homework help, activities, and experiments—all enhanced by the stunning photography that has brought National Geographic worldwide acclaim.

ePALS Classroom Exchange

http://www.epals.com

Close to 200 countries are involved in this cross-cultural exchange designed to dispel stereotypes and foster global understanding. Students and teachers are able to connect with others around the world in a school-safe environment with built-in language instruction.

Economics

Content Background Information

U.S. Department of the Treasury

http://www.treas.gov

The Treasury Department offers a wealth of information about taxes, personal finance, and financial markets. The section entitled Researchers, Students, and Teachers presents information about currency, FAQs about the Treasury, and a virtual tour and history of the Treasury. A special For the Kids section has links to other government sites that support or are connected to the Treasury.

Lesson Plans, Strategies, and Materials

Economic Education Web

http://ecedweb.unomaha.edu/home.htm

This portal site offers a wide variety of materials for teaching economics. Teachers will find the K-12 Teach section especially useful since they can search for lessons by standards, concepts, or grade level. The Support button leads visitors to additional economic resources by grade level.

Economics and Geography Lessons for 32 Children's Books

http://www.mcps.k12.md.us/curriculum/socialstd/Econ_Geog.html

This creative site from the Montgomery (Maryland) County Public Schools provides teaching ideas for teaching economics content using 32 different children's books. As an example, the concepts of Production, Scarcity, and Supply and Demand can be taught through the engaging book *Abuela's Weave.*

The Educator's Reference Desk: Economics

http://www.eduref.org/cgi-bin/print.cgi/Resources/Subjects/Social_Studies/Economics.html

Resources on this site are arranged by lesson plans, Internet sites, and organizations. Clicking on the EduRef Lesson Plans takes you to dozens of lessons and activities that break down complex economic topics into manageable pieces.

Money Instructor

http://www.moneyinstructor.com/

This website helps in teaching about money skills using reading, math, vocabulary, and other primary concepts. Most of the lesson plans, downloadable handouts, interactive games, and coloring sheets are suitable for elementary school use.

National Council on Economic Education

http://www.nationalcouncil.org

NCEE promotes economic literacy through a national network of educators and programs. Their self-proclaimed mission is to help students develop real-life economic skills they will need as adults: consumer awareness, employment information, and effective participation in the global economy. The site features resources such as lesson plans, interactive activities and games, and economic simulations, just to name a few.

Sites for Use in the Classroom with Children

Lemonade Stand

http://www.lemonadegame.com

Based on the computer game Lemonade Stand, this simulation allows students to engage in a capitalist venture. The High Game Scores feature encourages healthy competition among kids who participate.

U.S. Securities and Exchange Commission: For Students and Teachers

http://www.sec.gov/investor/students.shtml

The basics of saving and investing are explored on this site. Children can take an interactive quiz and use the savings calculator to find out how saving small sums today can add up to big money in the future. A guide for teachers provides discussion ideas as well as a five-unit curriculum, posters, and free downloadable publications. Links to other sites suitable for children are also provided.

The United States Mint's Site for Kids

http://www.usmint.gov/kids

This colorful website features games, cartoons, a time machine, and all sorts of information about coins past and present. The Teachers section provides lesson ideas and allows educators to submit their own successful plans.

Citizenship

Content Background Information

The Avalon Project

http://www.yale.edu/lawweb/avalon/avalon.htm

Maintained at Yale University, this site furnishes full-text documents that are critical for the study of American democracy. The documents are organized by time period, from pre-18th century to the 21st century. Examples include the Code of Hammurabi, the Articles of Confederation, and the September 11th Report.

Center for Civic Education

http://www.civiced.org/byrd

A federal mandate requires that every school—from kindergarten to postsecondary—provide instruction on the U.S. Constitution on September 17, Constitution Day and Citizenship Day. September 17 is the anniversary of the document's signing. This site offers free, ready-to-use lessons featuring discussion topics, exercises, readings, questions, and activities.

Public Agenda

http://www.publicagenda.org/

Public Agenda's nonpartisan Issue Guides distill facts and analysis from major news and public opinion sources and provides one of the most even-handed set of facts and analysis of such current events topics as welfare reform, environment, and crime.

Thomas

http://thomas.loc.gov

The Thomas system was put online by the Library of Congress at the beginning of the 104th Congress in January 1995. Since then, students and teachers of government have consulted this site to follow bills before Congress, monitor committee activity, read the *Congressional Record*, and easily search for public laws. While the main focus is the legislative branch, this site provides web links to all branches of government.

Lesson Plans, Strategies, and Materials

The American Promise

http://www.farmers.com/FarmComm/AmericanPromise

This program is designed to help teachers "bring democracy to life in their classrooms." Downloadable lesson plans and project ideas facilitate implementing the program in your school and community. The 170-page teaching guide, based on the public television series, can be ordered free of charge.

Center for Civic Education

http://www.civiced.org

The CCE is a nonpartisan educational corporation created to promote responsible citizenship. The Resources section provides sample lessons from the Center's textbooks and free classroom sets of We the People, a nationally acclaimed program on the U.S. Constitution and Bill of Rights for upper elementary students.

Civics Online

http://civics-online.org/teachers/

Civics Online has numerous lesson plans for all elementary grade levels, an interactive timeline of major events in American democracy, and a gateway to other civics websites.

FirstGov.gov

http://www.firstgov.gov/

This is the official U.S. gateway to all government information for citizens, businesses, and nongovernment organizations. The Reference section includes links to data and statistics, graphics and photos, and a host of federal laws including the Bill of Rights, Executive Orders, and Supreme Court decisions. The searchable database makes it easy to find specific laws.

U.S. Census Bureau

http://www.census.gov/dmd/www/teachers.html

The Census in Schools program provides lesson plans, teaching tools, resources, and professional development opportunities for educators. For elementary school teachers, lesson plans are divided into K–4 and 5–8 to aid in determining appropriateness. The teaching kits and maps are downloadable free of charge.

Sites for Use in the Classroom with Children

Ben's Guide to U.S. Government for Kids

http://bensguide.gpo.gov/

Benjamin Franklin guides children throughout this attractive, child-friendly portal site. Students learn how our government works, can access primary source materials, and learn how to carry out their civic responsibilities. The site can be accessed in age-appropriate ways by grade levels. A separate entryway for parents and teachers provides dozens of links to other government sites.

CIA's Homepage for Kids

http://www.cia.gov/cia/ciakids

The Central Intelligence Agency has a special K–5 grade Web page that offers background information on the organization's history and seal, the CIA Canine Corps, and the Aerial Photography Pigeons. Games include Geography Trivia, Break the Code, and Try a Disguise.

Federal Bureau of Investigation

http://www.fbi.gov/fbikids.htm

The FBI's children's page describes how the agency conducts crime investigation and prevention in the United States. Grade-sensitive games, lessons, and activities enable students to explore law enforcement in age-appropriate ways. Topics include safety tips, fingerprints, crime-fighting dogs, and forensics.

The Office of the Clerk: Kids in the House

http://clerkkids.house.gov

This interactive site teaches about the U.S. House of Representatives and its role in the legislative process. Students learn about lawmaking through virtual field trips, games, and a Time Traveler feature.

U.S. Department of Justice

http://www.usdoj.gov/kidspage/kids.htm

This Web page from the Department of Justice offers children in grades K–5 an array of resources related to the law, crime prevention, and civil rights. Topics include Internet safety, Cyberethics, and service dogs. Kids will especially enjoy the virtual field trips to federal court. A link for teachers and parents is also provided.

U.S. Department of State for Youth

http://future.state.gov

This K–12 Web page for the U.S. Department of State uses interactive technology to teach about foreign affairs and diplomacy, world geography, and current events. A special K–6 section allows students to learn more about the department and the Secretary of State while playing interactive games.

White House Kids

http://www.whitehouse.gov/kids

This engaging website teaches students about the lives of the presidents who have lived in the White House, provides a timeline of significant events in U.S. history, and challenges students through word games and quizzes. Young children will especially enjoy the historical ABCs, coloring pages, and photos of the family pets.

Justice for Kids and Youth

http://www.usdoj.gov/kidspage/

Designed for use with kids in a whole-class setting or at PC stations, this website introduces children to the court system and FBI. In addition, it has downloadable children's books that can be reproduced as basal text materials for learning about the court system.

Families, Personal Growth, and Development

Content Background Information

American Anthropological Association

http://www.aaanet.org/

The AAA offers educators a series of online brochures on a variety of anthropological topics. The section Anthropology in Education helps facilitate the integration of the field into K–12 settings. The Anthropological Resources page provides links to dozens of useful sites, and the Teaching About Race page gives excellent suggestions for the discussion of this potentially controversial issue.

American Psychological Association

http://www.apa.org

Teachers will appreciate the clear, easy-to-understand articles available under Psychology Topics. Clicking on the topic Children and Families, for example, yields a number of readings, press releases, and links to other resources.

ArchNet

http://archnet.asu.edu

ArchNet is a gateway site to virtual digs, electronic publications, and over 100 museums. Particularly useful is the Regions Web page that allows visitors to click on any portion of the map provided and be connected to a list of servers providing reports, images, and archaeological data.

Classics in the History of Psychology

http://psychclassics.yorku.ca

This virtual textbook provides full-text versions of the classic writings that make up the discipline of psychology. Full citations are provided as well as a link to the complete text. Searchable by author or topic.

Lesson Plans, Strategies, and Materials

The American Folklife Center

http://www.loc.gov/folklife/teachers/

This online guide includes a useful list of materials to incorporate folklife projects and programs. The searchable database can also be browsed by geographic area and subject. Many of the books, sound recordings, and audiovisual materials are available through various means accessible to teachers. Links to other websites are also provided.

Anthropology on the Internet for K–12

http://www.sil.si.edu/SILPublications/Anthropology-K12/anth-k12.htm

Maintained by the Smithsonian Institution, this gateway site includes an annotated list of anthropology-related websites. Links to other museums, virtual exhibits, and informative publications are easily accessed.

Scholastic: Teaching About Families

http://teacher.scholastic.com/lessonplans/unit_familyprek_books.htm

Maintained by Scholastic, the major educational publisher, this site features teacher-tested teaching ideas. Lessons and activities are broken down by grade level and include complete plans, stories, and suggestions for helpful children's storybooks to discuss the concept of family.

World Wise Schools

http://www.peacecorps.gov/wws/guides/looking/index.html

The Web page Looking at Ourselves and Others provides an excellent teacher's guide with lesson plans, activities, and stories that introduce students to the concept of culture. The lesson plans are broken down by grade level and aim to reduce prejudice by exploring and understanding the universal human characteristic of culture.

Sites for Use in the Classroom with Children

Brain: The World Inside Your Head

http://www.pfizer.com/brain/etour1.html

This attractive and informative site provides students with a virtual tour of the human brain. Students can enter through a variety of topics such as Mystery of the Mind, The Living Brain, and The Lightning Storm. Best for upper elementary students.

Just for Kids

http://www.urbanext.uiuc.edu/kids/index.html

This resource network allows children to explore a number of important topics such as environmental stewardship, responsible money management, and nutrition and health.

KidsPsych

http://www.kidspsych.org/index1.html

This "interactive web adventure for kids" is maintained by the American Psychological Association. Children can access the activities by age (ages 1–5 and ages 6–9). Teachers can click on the "about this activity" button to learn about the purpose of the activity and to get citations for further reading. The "info for parents" page is equally useful for teachers.

Neuroscience for Kids

http://faculty.washington.edu/chudler/neurok.html

Neuroscience for Kids allows students to explore the nervous system in an engaging, interactive way. High-quality graphics and humor peppered throughout appeal to children. The Experiments and Activities section features project ideas, brain and outside games, a coloring book, and a gallery of student projects.

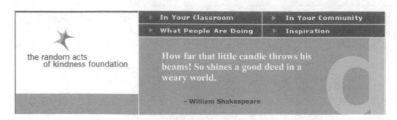

| | ▶ In Your Classroom | ▶ In Your Community |
| the random acts of kindness foundation | ▶ What People Are Doing | ▶ Inspiration |

How far that little candle throws his beams! So shines a good deed in a weary world.

- William Shakespeare

Reprinted with permission.

The Random Acts of Kindness Foundation

 http://www.actsofkindness.org/

This site promotes individual responsibility and sacrifice by providing activities, lesson plans, and documents for teachers to use in personal development and citizenship education.

CHECK THEM OUT!

The Companion Website at **www.prenhall.com/cruz** has **Bonus Links** that are not included in the textbook!

CHAPTER 9

Fine and Performing Arts

👉 **REMEMBER!**
Visit the Companion Website at **www.prenhall.com/cruz** for links to each website in this book.

Children's creative expression can be facilitated in a number of ways by using Internet resources. The following professional organizations and standards play an essential role in dance, music, theatre, and visual arts education and the development of your teacher practices.

ArtsEdge Website

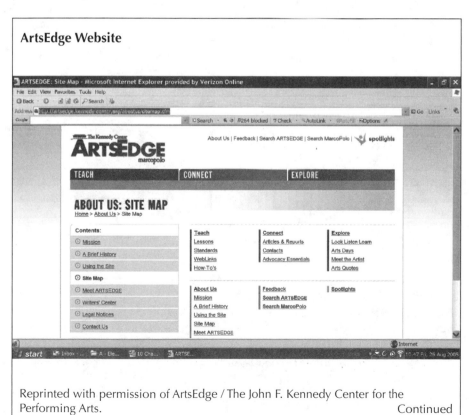

Reprinted with permission of ArtsEdge / The John F. Kennedy Center for the Performing Arts.

Continued

National Organizations and Standards on the Internet

Professional Organizations of Teachers of Fine and Performing Arts

National Art Education Association
http://www.naea-reston.org/

The National Association for Music Education
http://www.menc.org/

Educational Theatre Association
http://www.edta.org/

National Dance Education Organization
http://www.ndeo.org/

Related Organizations

American Alliance for Theatre & Education
http://www.aate.com/

The American Music Conference
http://www.amc-music.com/aboutus.htm

Americans for the Arts
http://www.artsusa.org

Arts Education Partnership
http://aep-arts.org/

Kennedy Center's ArtsEdge
http://artsedge.kennedy-center.org/

National Assembly of State Arts Agencies
http://www.nasaa-arts.org/

National Endowment for the Arts
http://arts.endow.gov/

American Choral Directors Association
http://acdaonline.org/

American String Teachers Association with National School Orchestra Association
http://www.astaweb.com/

National Dance Association
http://www.aahperd.org/nda/template.cfm?template=main.html

American Alliance for Health, Physical Education, Recreation and Dance
http://www.aahperd.org/index.html

National and State Standards

National Standards for Arts Education (Dance, Music, Visual Arts & Theatre)
http://artsedge.kennedy-center.org/teach/standards.cfm

National Standards for Music Education
http://www.menc.org/publication/books/standards.htm

INTASC Standards for Arts Teacher Education
http://www.ccsso.org/content/pdfs/ArtsStandards.pdf

Your **state standards** can be found at
http://edstandards.org/Standards.html or
http://www.aligntoachieve.org/AchievePhaseII/basic-search.cfm.

ERIC and GEM

ERIC, http://www.eric.ed.gov/ (see Chapter 3), has almost 4,000 online articles;
search for "arts, music, theater, or dance" AND "elementary education."

GEM, http://www.thegateway.org/browse (see Chapter 3), has over 10,000 possible
lesson plans in arts for use at the elementary school level.

Although the fine and performing arts have been the victim of drastic budget cuts
in public education in the last decade, teachers understand the importance and
benefits of using these art forms in their classrooms. In this chapter, the best
websites for dance, music, theatre, and visual arts instruction are presented. Two
websites in particular deserve mention as being all-inclusive:

> **ArtsEdge** at http://artsedge.kennedy-center.org/aboutus/sitemap.cfm, developed and maintained by the Kennedy Center, includes links to hundreds of lesson plans related to the arts. Teachers will appreciate that helpful grade and topic guides are listed alongside the titles.

> **Knowledge Network Explorer: Arts** at (http://www.kn.pacbell.com/wired/bluewebn/categories.cfm#6), organized by subject area, offers links to thousands of sites. The Arts section lists topics such as architecture, music, the performing arts, and the visual arts.

Dance

**NATIONAL DANCE
ASSOCIATION**

Reprinted with permission.

Content Background Information

Ballet Notes

http://www.balletmet.org/balletnotes.html

Two alphabetical indexes (one by choreographer and one by ballet title) allows users to gather
synopses and historical information about the most famous ballet works.

History of Dance

http://www.centralhome.com/ballroomcountry/history.htm

Brief histories are provided of each of the most widely known forms of dance, including the waltz, mambo, tango, swing, and flamenco.

Sapphire Swan Dance Directory

http://www.sapphireswan.com/dance

Although this is a sponsored commercial site, its online directory lists virtually every dance form imaginable. Links then take you to other sites that provide historical information, descriptions of the dances, and in some cases, animated clips.

Lesson Plans, Strategies, and Materials

Great Performances: Dance

http://www.pbs.org/wnet/gperf/genre/dance.html

This excellent PBS site offers teachers multimedia clips, educational resources, and an opportunity for dialogue. Although lesson plans for teachers are mostly at the middle and secondary school level, many can be easily modified for elementary school use.

PE Central: Dance Lesson Ideas

http://www.pecentral.org/lessonideas/dance/danceindex.asp

Teachers can access lessons by categories such as American folk dances, international dances, and rhythm activities. The National Dance Standards are also included.

Teachnology: Dance Lesson Plans

http://www.teach-nology.com/teachers/lesson_plans/arts/dance

A great collection of lesson plans on a wide variety of dance forms such as African American dance, line dancing, and creating movement through literature. There is also a teaching discussion section where users can log on by the grade level span most pertinent to them (e.g., K–2, 3–5).

Sites for Use in the Classroom with Children

A Dancer's Journal

http://artsedge.kennedy-center.org/marthagraham/index.htm

Most appropriate for upper elementary school grades, this website chronicles the first year of a new dancer in the Martha Graham Dance Company. Set up in the form of a school locker, users can read the dancer's journal, hear accompanying music, and view video clips of the dances.

Music

The Society for American Music

Society for American Music

http://www.voicesacrosstime.org/guide/songgrid.html

The Society for American Music has excellent resources for elementary school teachers. The above link takes you to *Voices Across Time*, which is organized by historical eras derived from the National History Standards and themes adapted from the National Social Studies Standards. Each song can be played and the lyrics can be downloaded.

The National Association for Music Education

http://www.menc.org

With the mission to "advance music education by encouraging the study and making of music by all," NAME's website offers online periodicals, resources, conference information, and professional development opportunities. The Links page provides dozens of links to other arts-related websites.

Content Background Information

American Music on the World Wide Web

http://www.american-music.org/resources/ResourcesOnWeb.htm

Organized by type of music (e.g., popular, sacred, and classical), users can not only learn more about American music but also hear samples of each genre.

Arizona Opera

http://www.azopera.com/learn.php

For teachers who want to learn more about opera, its terminology, and history, the Opera Resource Center offers synopses, pronunciation guides, and historical biographies. There is also a kids' section with games and activities that both entertain and educate.

Essentials of Music

http://www.essentialsofmusic.com/main.html

This website highlights "the best music of every period" and features background information on the six main musical eras, a glossary, biographies of composers, and a collection of over 200 audio clips.

Instrument Encyclopedia

http://www.si.umich.edu/chico/instrument

Teachers can learn more about the familiar and some of the more exotic musical instruments. Users can browse by the four major instrument types (percussion, strings, winds, and electronic) or by geographic region.

Lesson Plans, Strategies, and Materials

The Educator's Reference Desk: Music Lesson Plans

http://www.eduref.org/cgi-bin/lessons.cgi/Arts/Music

These teacher-created lessons are helpfully organized by grade level. Topics are wide-ranging, including Beethoven, reggae, salsa music, and funk.

K–12 Resources for Music Educators

http://www.isd77.k12.mn.us/resources/staffpages/shirk/k12.music.html

The section called Sites for Classroom Music Teachers is especially helpful, containing links to multimedia sites, downloadable songs, and ideas for classroom instruction. More detailed sections for choral teachers, band leaders, and so on are also provided.

Music Education Resources Idea Library

http://www.angelfire.com/nb2/musicedresources

Don't be put off by this plain-looking site. It nonetheless is an extensive collection of links arranged alphabetically by topic covering all the major music themes that would be of interest to a music teacher.

Rock and Roll Hall of Fame

http://www.rockhall.com/programs/plans.asp

Lesson plans created by educators during past Summer Teacher Institutes are listed on this site by topic. Creative ideas include popular music and the civil rights movement, using rock to teach literature, and using hip hop to introduce allusion.

Songs for Teaching

http://www.songsforteaching.com/index.htm

Many ideas for using music and songs to teach concepts and skills in a variety of content areas. Curriculum areas include mathematics, reading, social studies, and science.

Sites for Use in the Classroom with Children

ArtsAlive: Music

http://www.artsalive.ca/en/mus/index.asp

Sponsored by the National Arts Centre in Canada, ArtsAlive provides information about orchestral music, great composers and conductors, and musical instruments. The Activities and Games page challenges students with quizzes about music, tests their musical memory, and allows them to create their own musical score.

Children's Music Web

http://www.childrensmusic.org

This nonprofit organization is for teachers and parents as well as children. The Resources for Kids page allows children to listen to musical selections, make their own CDs, learn how to do sound effects, and create their own radio show.

Dallas Symphony Orchestra

http://www.dsokids.com/2001/rooms/musicroom.asp

Reprinted with permission from the Dallas Symphony Orchestra.

The Dallas Symphony Orchestra has done a fine job of making classical music accessible and understandable to children. Students will find educational games, ideas for making their own instruments, and the opportunity to hear a wide variety of instruments. The Teacher's Lounge offers lesson plans, activities, content background on composers and instruments, and yet more links to other sites.

The New York Philharmonic KidZone

http://www.nyphilkids.org/main.phtml

This attractive site offers a musician's lounge, a composers' gallery, an instrument laboratory, and a game room. In the game room children can learn about instruments, composers, and even make their own instrument.

San Francisco Symphony for Kids

http://www.sfskids.org

This site provides information about instruments, a music basics tutorial, and a listing of family programs and activities at the San Francisco Symphony.

Sesame Street Music Works

http://www.sesameworkshop.org/sesamestreet/music

Children can listen to a variety of musical types in the Music Zone, including opera, global rhythms, and perennial childhood favorites. On Sesame Street Radio children can listen to popular songs from the TV show. Music Works offers tips for educators and parents to help children learn from and appreciate music.

Theatre

Reprinted with permission.

Educational Theatre Association

http://www.edta.org

The ETA publishes a magazine and quarterly journal for teachers. A searchable engine allows you to find articles in *Teaching Theatre* and then download them for free as PDF files.

Content Background Information

Story Arts

http://www.storyarts.org

This website explains how storytelling can be used in the classroom. A series of articles and essays help educators understand how storytelling can be used to build academic success and develop emotional well-being. Also included is a collection of illustrative lesson plans and suggested materials.

Theatre History

http://www.theatrehistory.com

Theatre in each major time period in history and geographic region is discussed through a series of articles and essays. Users are also provided with additional links to other helpful sites.

Lesson Plans, Strategies, and Materials

The Costume Page

http://www.costumepage.org

A collection of over 2,000 links providing information on historical costumes, theatrical costumes, ethnic garb, and ideas for materials.

Creative Drama and Theatre Education

http://www.creativedrama.com

Elementary school teachers will appreciate the use of folk and fairy tales for creative dramatic play. Classroom ideas, theatre games, and plays for performance can be accessed by teachers. Sample lesson plans for dramatizing children's books are also provided.

The Drama Teacher's Resource Room

http://www.sasktelwebsite.net/erachi

Teachers can find creative activities and lesson plans on this site as well as articles on costuming, props, and scenery. The Great Drama Links section offers even more extensive information.

Learning Through Storytelling

http://www.turnerlearning.com/turnersouth/storytelling/index.html

Using stories and fables from the U.S. South, this site offers many suggestions for using stories and storytelling in the classroom. Lesson plans and a helpful biography are included.

Sites for Use in the Classroom with Children

Seattle Children's Theatre

http://www.sct.org

SCT produces classic children's stories and new works for the theatre. On their website, children can view video clips of recent performances such as *Alexander and the Terrible, Horrible, No Good, Very Bad Day*, and *A Year with Frog and Toad*.

Visual Arts

National Gallery of Art Teaching Resource

Content Background Information

About Life: The Photographs of Dorothea Lange

http://www.getty.edu/art/exhibitions/lange/index.html

This stunning visual gallery of Dorothea Lange's photography not only can be used to teach about the Great Depression, but also provides information on Lange as an artist and a video gallery with "behind the scenes" looks at making art.

Africa: The Art of a Continent

http://artnetweb.com/guggenheim/africa

The Guggenheim Museum's website on African art is both visually arresting and incredibly informative. The collection includes works ranging from tools and rock art of early humankind to contemporary pieces. Artwork can be browsed by geographic region as well as by a clickable map that provides a brief history of each region.

The American Museum of Photography

http://www.photography-museum.com

This ongoing collection of photography exhibits is wide-ranging in terms of scope and variety. A guided tour gives visitors an overview of the collection and its resources.

Art History Resources on the Web

http://witcombe.bcpw.sbc.edu/ARTHLinks.html

This exhaustive site includes topics ranging from prehistoric art to 21st century art. Links to galleries, images, and projects provide users with a wide range of art resources.

Art Studio Chalkboard

http://www2.evansville.edu/studiochalkboard

This resource focuses on the technical fundamentals of perspective, shading, color, and painting. Although detailed in its scope and discussion, terms and processes are clearly explained and easily understood.

Artcyclopedia

http://www.artcyclopedia.com

Billed as "the guide to great art on the Internet," this website features biographies, articles, glossaries, visuals, and much more.

ArtLex Art Dictionary

http://www.artlex.com

Close to 4,000 terms are defined in this online dictionary. Definitions are supported with thousands of images, pronunciation guides, and pertinent quotations and references.

Exploring Themes in American Art

http://www.nga.gov/education/american/aasplash.htm

The National Gallery of Art supplies educators with a wealth of information on abstraction, landscape painting, portraiture, still life, and other topics. This teaching resource also offers images, biographies, and a glossary.

Lesson Plans, Strategies, and Materials

Arts Connected

http://www.artsconnected.org

The Minneapolis Institute of Arts offers this wonderful resource for teachers. In the For Your Classroom section you will find a searchable educational database that breaks down lessons and activities by K–3, 4–5, and 6–8 grades. A Teacher's Guide is downloadable as a PDF file. Children will also love the Playground and Toolkit.

ArtsEdNet

http://www.getty.edu/education

The J. Paul Getty Trust maintains this site, which offers free lesson plans, curriculum ideas, image galleries, and an online discussion forum. The lessons are sorted by grade level and include topics such as African American art, arts of India, and women artists of the Americas.

Kathy Schrock's Guide for Educators: Art and Architecture

http://school.discovery.com/schrockguide/arts/artarch.html

This selective list of art sites includes links to museums, education materials, and lesson plans.

Kinder Art

http://www.kinderart.com

Offering over 1,000 art lesson plans, this site features a search engine as well as a master list for browsing. There are also ideas for bulletin boards, crafts projects, and tips for teachers.

National Gallery of Art

http://www.nga.gov/education

The NGA offers a Teaching Resources section on their website with two valuable supports for elementary school teachers: NGA Classroom and NGA Loan Program. In the former, you will find lessons and resources that can be accessed by topic, artist, or curriculum area. The Loan Program allows teachers to borrow audiovisual materials and teaching packets at no charge.

Sites for Use in the Classroom with Children

ArtEdventures

http://www.sanford-artedventures.com/index.html

In addition to an online gallery, this site contains resources for creating, studying, and teaching art. The interactive game section includes activities for both teachers and students. The breadth of topics is wide, from cave art to contemporary architecture.

Artgames

http://www.albrightknox.org/artgames/index.html

This visually arresting site features an interactive art experience for children ages 4 to 12. Students can learn about color, portraits, still lifes, and landscapes. Your Own Studio allows users to create colorful, abstract works.

Crayola Creativity Central

http://www.crayola.com

This colorful and entertaining site includes ideas for parents and teachers in addition to activities for kids. Users can create cards, take a virtual field trip to the Crayola factory, and get scores of ideas for arts and crafts projects.

 CHECK THEM OUT!

The Companion Website at **www.prenhall.com/cruz** has **Bonus Links** that are not included in the textbook!

CHAPTER 10

Health and Physical Education

> **☞ REMEMBER!**
> Visit the Companion Website at **www.prenhall.com/cruz** for links to each website in this book.

The following professional organizations, journals, and standards play an essential role in health and physical education and the development of your teacher practices.

The American Alliance for Health, Physical Education, Recreation and Dance

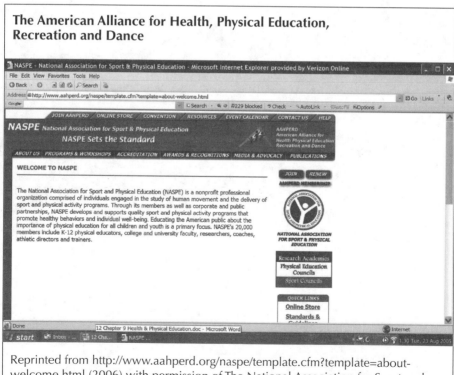

Reprinted from http://www.aahperd.org/naspe/template.cfm?template=about-welcome.html (2006) with permission of The National Association for Sport and Physical Education (NASPE), 1900 Association Drive, Reston, VA 20191-1599.

National Organizations and Standards on the Internet

Professional Organizations for Teachers of Health and Physical Education

National Association for Sport and Physical Education
http://www.aahperd.org/naspe/template.cfm?template=main.html

American Association for Health Education
http://www.aahperd.org/aahe/

The American Alliance for Health, Physical Education, Recreation and Dance
http://www.aahperd.org/aahperd/template.cfm

Related Organizations

American Association for Active Lifestyles and Fitness
http://www.aahperd.org/aaalf/template.cfm?template=main.html

American Association for Leisure and Recreation
http://www.aahperd.org/aalr/template.cfm?template=main.html

National Association for Girls and Women in Sport
http://www.aahperd.org/nagws/template.cfm?template=main.html

National Dance Association
http://www.aahperd.org/nda/template.cfm?template=main.html

Research Consortium
http://www.aahperd.org/research/template.cfm?template=main.html

National and State Standards

National Standards for Physical Education
http://www.aahperd.org/NASPE/template.cfm?template=publications-
nationalstandards.html

National Health Education Standards
http://www.aahperd.org/aahe/pdf_files/standards.pdf
Your **state standards** can be found at
http://edstandards.org/Standards.html.

ERIC and GEM

ERIC, http://www.eric.ed.gov/ (see Chapter 3), has almost 4,000 online articles;
search for "health" and "physical education" AND "elementary education."

GEM, http://www.thegateway.org/browse (see Chapter 3), has over 9,000 possible
lesson plans in health and physical education for use at the elementary school level.

Health Education

Content Background Information

Healthy People 2010

http://www.healthypeople.gov/BeHealthy/

Healthy People is a U.S. federal government initiative that challenges individuals, communities,
and professionals to take specific steps to ensure that good health and long life are
enjoyed by all. This site includes a full-color book that provides the kind of background

information needed to teach health-related issues and an A–Z listing of health issues that provides background content information and links on such issues as drug abuse and diabetes.

KidsHealth for Kids

http://www.kidshealth.org/kid/

Reprinted with permission.

KidsHealth has separate areas for kids and parents—each with its own design, age-appropriate content, and tone. There are literally thousands of in-depth features, articles, animations, games, and resources—all original and all developed by experts in the health of children and teens.

Centers for Disease Control and Prevention: Health Promotion

http://www.cdc.gov/node.do/id/0900f3ec80059b1a

The Center for Disease Control and Prevention has a variety of resources that can be used in the classroom.

healthfinder

http://www.healthfinder.gov/hg/files/?id=_2_Diseases_%20Conditions%20and%20Injuries

healthfinder also has an A–Z list of all the major diseases with an explanation of the causes, preventions, and treatments.

Lesson Plans, Strategies, and Materials

PBS TeacherSource: Health & Fitness

http://www.pbs.org/teachersource/health.htm

PBS has lesson plans that are cataloged by grade level on topics such as body system, health, and aging.

PE Central: Health Lesson Plans

http://www.pecentral.org/lessonideas/health/healthlp.asp

PE Central is a comprehensive site for both PE and health with detailed lessons for both PE teachers and teachers in other disciplines who want to integrate PE and health into their other subjects.

Communities and Schools Promoting Health

http://www.safehealthyschools.org/lessonplansintro.htm

This Canadian website has lesson plans for physical education activities and health education.

HealthTeacher

http://www.healthteacher.com/lessonguides/nutrition.asp

HealthTeacher has lesson plans on nutrition, alcohol, drug and tobacco abuse, personal mental hygiene, and more. However, there is a fee for the lesson plans.

PBS Kids

http://pbskids.org/arthur/parentsteachers/lesson/health/

This health curriculum guide is designed for teachers. Each unit explores a different early childhood health topic, offering background information, a featured ARTHUR show, classroom activities, recommended books, and in many cases, family activity sheets in English, Spanish, Chinese, Tagalog, and Vietnamese.

The Alabama Learning Exchange

http://alex.state.al.us/search.php?fa_submit=PLANS

At ALEX, you can select health and PE and your grade level for access to lesson plans compiled by the Alabama Department of Education.

Sites for Use in the Classroom with Children

Department of Health and Human Services: Interactive Menu Planner

http://hin.nhlbi.nih.gov/menuplanner/menu.cgi

The National Heart, Lung, and Blood Institute provides a menu planner and a body mass calculator that teachers can use in the classroom.

KidsHealth: How the Body Works

http://www.kidshealth.org/kid/body/mybody.html

This site provides a grade-appropriate explanation of how the body works.

STARBRIGHT World

http://www.starbright.org/projects/sbworld/

STARBRIGHT World is a safe and secure online community where kids and teens living with serious illnesses can connect with each other. Kids on SBW can chat, read and post to bulletin boards, e-mail, search for friends with similar illnesses, participate in fun events and contests, surf prescreened websites, and play games.

PBS: Kid-Friendly Medical Dictionary

http://www.pbs.org/parents/talkingwithkids/health/med_index_1.html

PBS developed this dictionary of common medical terms from *allergies* to *X-ray machine* for use with or by children.

Physical Education

Content Background Information

McREL: Health and Physical Education

http://www.mcrel.org/lesson-plans/health/index.asp

The Mid-continent Research for Education and Learning offers lesson plan ideas, advocacy of health and physical education, and links to other websites supporting health and PE.

PE Central: Adapted Physical Education

http://www.pecentral.org/adapted/adaptedmenu.html

For students with disabilities to enjoy an active lifestyle, teachers need to differentiate instruction. This site explains the goals of adapted physical education.

National Association for Sport and Physical Education

http://www.aahperd.org/naspe/template.cfm?template=position-papers.html

The NASPE has position papers analyzing issues and stating their positions on such topics as recess, dodge ball, and so on.

Lesson Plans, Strategies, and Materials

PE Central

http://www.pecentral.org/index.html

This comprehensive website has hundreds of lesson plans that are integrated with other subjects such as mathematics, stand-alone activities, tips on classroom management during PE activities, lining up approaches, and more.

Reprinted with permission from PE Central.

NASPE Teacher's Toolbox

http://www.aahperd.org/naspe/template.cfm?template=teachers_toolbox.html

Click on Toolbox at the National Association for Sport and Physical Education and every month you will have a fitness calendar to send home with your students, bulletin board ideas, information about the nation's health observances, and the newest resource materials.

Sports Media

http://www.sports-media.org/links/data/index.html

Sports Media has a number of lesson plans designed for coaching in specific sports and other links that provide content information at a more expert level about specific sports.

Physical Education Lesson Plan Page

http://members.tripod.com/~pazz/lesson.html

This site provides a large number of creative activities with detailed explanations of how to set up the PE activity.

Active Energizers

http://www.ncpe4me.com/energizers.html

Energizers are classroom-based physical activities that integrate physical activity with academic concepts. These are short (about 10 minutes) activities that classroom teachers can use to provide activity to children.

The Lesson Plans Page

http://www.lessonplanspage.com/PEK1.htm

The Lesson Plans Page has a large number of lesson plans that are stand-alone activities, but also includes activities that are extensions of classroom learning experiences in other disciplines.

Sites for Use in the Classroom with Children. Due to the nature of physical education, pertinent sites in this category are included under health education.

 CHECK THEM OUT!
The Companion Website at **www.prenhall.com/cruz** has **Bonus Links** that are not included in the textbook!

CHAPTER 11

World Languages

A wide range of educational reports have called for the teaching and advancement of world languages in the elementary grades. Whether you teach an actual foreign language course at your school or simply introduce vocabulary and sayings to your students, the following professional organizations, journals, and standards play an essential role in world language education and the development of your teacher practices.

The American Council on the Teaching of Foreign Languages

Reprinted with permission of the American Council on the Teaching of Foreign Languages.

National Organizations and Standards on the Internet

Professional Organizations for Teachers of Foreign Language

American Council on the Teaching of Foreign Languages
http://www.actfl.org/

Modern Language Association
http://www.mla.org

American Association for Applied Linguistics
http://www.aaal.org/

Related Organizations

American Association of Teachers of French
http://www.frenchteachers.org/

American Association of Teachers of German
http://www.aatg.org

American Association of Teachers of Italian
http://www.italianstudies.org/aati/

American Association of Teachers of Spanish and Portuguese
http://www.aatsp.org/ScriptContent/Index.cfm

The American Classical League
http://www.aclclassics.org/

American Councils for International Education
http://www.americancouncils.org/home.asp?PageID=1

The Association for Language Learning
http://www.all-languages.org.uk

Teachers of English to Speakers of Other Languages, Inc.
http://www.tesol.org

American Association of Teachers of Slavic and Eastern European Languages
http://aatseel.org/

American Association of Teachers of Arabic
http://www.wm.edu/aata/

The Association of Teachers of Japanese
http://www.colorado.edu/ealld/atj/

Chinese Language Teachers Association
http://clta.osu.edu/

National and State Standards

Standards for Foreign Language Learning: Preparing for the 21st Century were first published in 1996 and again in 1999; see
http://www.actfl.org/index.cfm?weburl=/public/articles/details.cfm?id=33.

Your **state standards** can be found at
http://edstandards.org/Standards.html or
http://www.aligntoachieve.org/AchievePhaseII/basic-search.cfm.

Continued

ERIC and GEM

ERIC, http://www.eric.ed.gov/ (see Chapter 3), has almost 1,700 online articles; search for "foreign language education" AND "elementary education."
GEM, http://www.thegateway.org/browse (see Chapter 3), has over 800 possible lesson plans in languages for use at the elementary school level.

Although space does not permit us to cover each world language that might be taught in your school, the following links will provide you with a good starting point in teaching the most popular foreign languages in the United States and will direct you to other, less taught world languages. The first section features general multilingual sites that provide content background information, lesson plans, and instructional strategies and resources; a section on sites for use in the classroom is also included. Following the general section are links to the specific languages of Spanish, French, German, and Japanese. (Note: Information and resources regarding English Language Learners can be found in Chapter 12, Meeting the Needs of Diverse Learners.)

General Multilingual Sites

Clip Art Collection for Foreign Language Instruction

http://www.sla.purdue.edu/fll/JapanProj/FLClipart

This page contains clip art that can be used by foreign language instructors free of charge. Drawings are designed to be as culturally and linguistically neutral as possible. To simplify searching, the clip art is grouped in useful categories such as food and drinks, people and animals, and buildings and places.

NewsDirectory

http://www.ecola.com

This multilingual site allows users to access thousands of newspapers around the world—in both native languages as well as English translations. You can browse by country, region, or subject.

FLTeach

http://www.cortland.edu/flteach

The Foreign Language Teaching Forum focuses on foreign language teaching methods for all levels and all languages. It includes an archive, FAQs, updates on important legislative initiatives, and a bulletin board for users.

Foreign Language Teaching Forum

Intercultural E-Mail Classroom Connections

http://www.iecc.org/

IECC is a free service that helps teachers link with partners in other countries for e-mail classroom pen pals and other project exchanges. The K–12 forum is especially geared for primary and secondary school teachers.

The Internet TESL Journal

http://iteslj.org/

This online resource is updated monthly and includes scholarly articles and papers, lesson plans, classroom handouts and quizzes, and a variety of teaching ideas and links to other sites.

Internet Activities for Foreign Language Classes

http://www.clta.net/lessons

This website, maintained by the California Language Teachers Association, includes Web lessons, hundreds of activities, and links to authentic documents for use in the classroom.

Knowledge Network Explorer: Foreign Language

http://www.kn.pacbell.com/wired/bluewebn/contentarea.cfm?cid=6

Scroll down this award-winning site to the Foreign Language Section. There you will find links to the most common languages as well as American Sign Language, Classical Languages, and picture dictionaries.

Language Links

http://polyglot.lss.wisc.edu/lss/lang/langlink.html

This gateway site provides links to additional resources for the teaching of a large variety of world languages. The Teaching with the Web feature offers pedagogical strategies, Web activities, class lessons, and related publications.

Language Materials Project

http://www.lmp.ucla.edu/

Maintained by UCLA, this website supports the instruction of "less commonly taught languages." Users can select a language, materials, and a level for customized assistance.

Lesson Plans and Resources for ESL, Bilingual and Foreign Language Teachers

http://www.csun.edu/%7Ehcedu013/eslindex.html

This excellent website, maintained by a California State University professor, provides hundreds of links to other useful sites that contain lesson plans and resources, study abroad opportunities, and educational standards and frameworks.

Super Language Sites

http://www.uni.edu/becker

Out of the University of Northern Iowa, this website provides links to resources for a wide variety of world languages, including dictionaries, currency converters, free translation services, and online tutorials.

Sites for Use in the Classroom with Children

Fonetiks

http://fonetiks.org

This free, online pronunciation guide helps users with pronunciation in various languages. Pronunciation samples from native speakers are provided as well as common sentence patterns.

Little Explorers Picture Dictionary

http://www.enchantedlearning.com/Dictionary.html

This fun picture dictionary for kids allows users to choose a letter, see over 770 entries, and visit a related website.

Clue Word: Multilingual Word Puzzles and Games

http://www.clueword.com/cwhome.htm

This site includes a variety of games and puzzles designed to build vocabulary in various languages. Most appropriate for elementary-aged students are hangman, word find, and jumble words.

Songs for Learning New Languages

http://www.songsforteaching.com/languages.htm

Links to dozens of languages are provided on this multilingual site. Lyrics as well as audio files (to hear the songs and music) are included.

Sounds of the World's Animals

http://www.georgetown.edu/faculty/ballc/animals/animals.html

Although animals around the world make the same sounds, children are delighted to learn how different languages express each sound. Users can explore the sounds by either animal or language.

Spanish

ALA Great Websites for Kids: En Español

http://www.ala.org/gwstemplate.cfm?section=greatwebsites&template=/cfapps/gws/displaysection.cfm&sec=20

This portal site is particularly useful because it can be browsed by grade level (pre-K, elementary, and middle). All sites are kid friendly and allow students to practice their Spanish skills.

Bilingual Links for Kids and Teachers

http://members.tripod.com/~hamminkj/bilingue.html

A bilingual (Spanish/English) website catering to children ages 5 to 10. Provides stories, poetry, games, and links to other kid-friendly sites.

Centro Barahona

http://www.csusm.edu/csb/

The Recommended Books in Spanish feature is an excellent way to identify Spanish-language picture books for the elementary classroom. Teachers can search for books by specific grade level, age, and country.

Don Quijote

http://www.donquijote.org/pdd

In addition to building vocabulary while playing games in Spanish, this site also offers popular sayings, jokes in Spanish, and a verb conjugator.

El Alfabeto Español

http://www.comsewogue.k12.ny.us/showcase2000/falci/introduction.htm

Although quite simple, this is a good first introduction to the Spanish alphabet. Colorful cartoons and pictures for each letter of the alphabet enhance the alphabet and language development.

Españolé

http://www.espanole.org

This website is for Spanish-language teachers and their students, including learning activities and a special section on Hispanic Americans.

Internet Familia

http://www.familia.cl

The section for children, Niños, provides students with the opportunity to explore music, animals, nature, sports, and a whole host of other topics in Spanish.

LatinWorld: Kids

http://www.latinworld.com/special/kids.html

This bilingual site offers a wide variety of links for children, including Spanish-language stories, games, and online magazines.

Learn Spanish

http://studyspanish.com/freesite.htm

Reprinted with permission.

This online tutorial offers both free and membership services. The free site includes vocabulary building, travel help, idiom information, and verb drills.

Spanish Class Online

http://www.spanishclassonline.com

This site includes a wide array of free activities, classroom resources, and links to dictionaries, free translation services, and information about culture and countries.

Spanish Grammar Exercises

http://www.colby.edu/~bknelson/exercises/index.html

By using stories, images, songs, and guided readings, users learn about pronouns, interrogative words, regular and irregular tenses, and much more.

Songs for Teaching: Spanish Songs

http://www.songsforteaching.com/spanishsongs.htm

Using these songs, children can learn the numbers, the alphabet, colors, parts of the body, and much more. All include the lyrics and most include an audio file as well.

TeachSpanish.com

http://www.teachspanish.com

This site functions as a teacher exchange site for lesson plans and teaching ideas. The Country Resources section provides a wealth of information about Spanish-speaking countries. Students can also access the free electronic translator.

Webspañol

http://www.geocities.com/Athens/Thebes/6177

A great variety of interactive activities help users determine their level of Spanish proficiency, learn colorful Spanish idioms, and solve riddles in Spanish.

French

Songs for Teaching: French Songs

http://www.songsforteaching.com/frenchsongs.htm

This is a wonderful collection of children's songs designed to teach elementary vocabulary and language concepts. In addition to the French lyrics provided, audio files are included in most cases. Songs are helpfully organized by topics.

Le Journal des Enfants

http://www.jde.fr

This online French-language magazine gives children the opportunity to practice their skills while using student-appropriate contemporary issues and stories.

Launch Site for French

http://www.uga.edu/~romlan/rapports/launch.htm

A useful listing of annotated hyperlinks to sites for the study of French and francophone cultures.

Tennessee Bob's Famous French Links

http://www.utm.edu/departments/french/french.html

A one-stop site for the teaching of the French language, including links to French-language books, art, music, film, and French culture across the curriculum and in everyday life.

Reprinted with permission.

Why Learn French

http://french.about.com/od/whylearnfrench/

The links on this website enable teachers to explain the many benefits of learning French. Facts and figures about the French language, celebrities who speak French, and word games in French are all featured.

German

AATG Teaching Resources

Reprinted with permission.

http://grow.aatg.org/index.html

This gateway site features links to Web resources, learning activities, lesson plans, project ideas, and no-cost online German courses.

Songs for Teaching: German Songs

http://www.songsforteaching.com/germansongs.htm

A collection of songs in German appropriate for elementary classroom usage. In addition to the lyrics, audio clips are also provided.

Learn German Online

http://www.learn-german-online.net

This site focuses on "practical life" language skills and contains information on German for travelers, business etiquette, and German culture in general. Additionally, there are links to interactive sites, audio files, and suggestions for literature and film.

Learn German at About.com

http://german.about.com

Featuring a variety of activities for English speakers learning German, this website explains German noun suffixes and gender, grammar, and pronunciation. Word games and listening resources are also included.

Japanese

AskAsia: Adult-Free Zone

http://www.askasia.org/adult_free_zone/afz_frame.htm

Designed for use by children, this website features language and song activities, a virtual gallery of student art, and an e-pals school exchange service.

E. L. Easton: Languages Online (Japanese)

http://eleaston.com/languages.html

Although not visually appealing, this site nonetheless provides excellent links to other sites that focus on Japanese characters, grammar, quizzes, readings, and even Japanese audio commercials.

Japanese-Online.com

http://www.japanese-online.com

Although this website has a Members Only section, membership is free. It offers a series of Japanese-language lessons complete with dialogues, vocabulary, grammar, and sound files.

Kids Web Japan

http://web-japan.org/kidsweb/index.html

Developed specifically for children, this site includes a cookbook for kids, a culture corner, and a "say it in Japanese" section. This entertaining site is a good introduction for children to Japanese language and culture.

Resources for Japanese Students and Educators

http://www.colorado.edu/ealld/atj/Japan_info/resource.html

This annotated list of links identifies study guides, teaching resources, audiovisual materials, and other databases that support the teaching of Japanese and Asian cultures.

Web Japan

http://web-jpn.org/kidsweb

Teachers will find this website, billed as a gateway for all things Japanese, very useful in gathering background information on Japanese history, geography, and culture.

 CHECK THEM OUT!

The Companion Website at **www.prenhall.com/cruz** has **Bonus Links** that are not included in the textbook!

CHAPTER 12

Meeting the Needs of Diverse Learners

☞**REMEMBER!**
Visit the Companion Website at **www.prenhall.com/cruz** for links to each website in this book.

Without question, our nation's classrooms are becoming increasingly diverse. The student body is made up of children from various nations, cultures, religions, languages, socioeconomic backgrounds, and ability levels. This diversity brings a richness and complexity that can pose both challenges and opportunities in the classroom. This chapter will help you identify some of the best websites to help you navigate and utilize the diversity present in your school. Due to the special nature of this chapter, its organization is different from the preceding ones: after identifying one major professional organization on the topic, the sites will be listed according to these categories:

- Learning Styles and Multiple Intelligences
- English Language Learners (ELL)
- Cultural Differences among Learners
- Gifted Education
- Inclusion and Mainstreaming of People with Disabilities
- At-Risk Youth and Children in Crisis
- Family Involvement in Education

LEARNING STYLES AND MULTIPLE INTELLIGENCES

The work that really brought the idea of multiple intelligences to the forefront of education is Howard Gardner's book *Frames of Mind* (New York: Basic Books, 1983). The theory resonates with many teachers who recognize that there are many different learning styles present in their classrooms and that a multiple intelligences approach helps all students learn and understand material. The following websites offer explanations, learning activities, and Internet resources.

Concept to Classroom: Tapping into Multiple Intelligences

http://www.thirteen.org/edonline/concept2class/mi/index.html

Produced by the Educational Broadcasting Corporation, this site provides excellent teacher background information. In addition to clearly explaining the theory of multiple intelligences, users can also view real-world examples, explore ideas for applying it to their own classrooms, and download implementation activities.

Howard Gardner

http://www.howardgardner.com

This site is excellent for teachers wishing to learn more about the educator most closely associated with the theory. The site also offers essays on the topic, FAQs, links to other sites, and a section on students conducting research.

Howard Gardner and MI Links

http://www.geocities.com/Athens/Column/7568/gardner.html

This site includes an extensive set of links related to multiple intelligences theory. Teachers will find scores of lesson plans, best practices, MI inventories, and articles on related topics.

Teaching to the Seven Multiple Intelligences

http://www.mitest.com

This helpful website provides sample curriculum units in various subject areas. Equally useful are the online tests for 8- to 12-year-olds, 13- to 18-year-olds, and adults.

Learning Disabilities Resources Community: Multiple Intelligence Inventory

http://www.ldrc.ca/projects/miinventory/miinventory.php

Each of the multiple intelligences dimensions are described and outlined on this site. Users can also and take an inventory and participate in an online workshop.

ENGLISH LANGUAGE LEARNERS (ELL)

According to the U.S. Department of Education's Office of English Language Acquisition, about 10 percent of our nation's pre-K through 12th grade students have limited English proficiency. Although Spanish-speaking children make up the majority of our English Language Learners (ELLs), virtually every country and language on Earth is represented somewhere in the United States. If you do a general search on this topic, it is alternately referred to as ESOL, TESOL, and LEP, just to name a few terms. The following websites will help you learn the lingo, identify resources, and create activities for your unique teaching needs.

Teachers of English to Speakers of Other Languages

http://www.tesol.org

TESOL is an international education association that facilitates the teaching of English to nonnative speakers. In addition to teacher essentials such as curriculum standards and professional development opportunities, the TESOL website also provides the latest news in legislation, position statements, and discussion of global issues.

Reprinted with permission from TESOL.

National Association for Bilingual Education

http://www.nabe.org/

NABE promotes educational excellence and equity for ELLs. An online news digest and magazine updates educators on legislation, research reports, and resources.

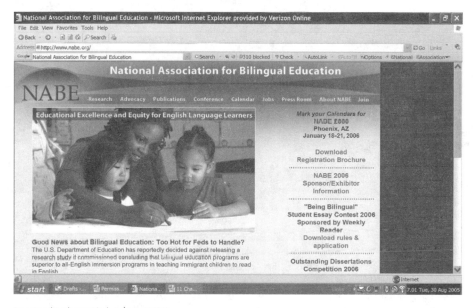

Reprinted with permission from NABE.

Bilingual Education

http://www.csun.edu/~hcedu013/eslbil.html

This gateway site for bilingual education facilitates access to a wide array of resources, centers, and lesson plans.

¡Colorín Colorado!

http://www.colorincolorado.org

This multimedia website is a service of PBS station WETA and is intended to support Spanish-speaking parents in helping their children learn to read. The interactive site features attractive illustrations and entertaining video clips of celebrities. Also included are downloadable resources for teachers to distribute to parents in their own communities.

Dave's ESL Café

http://www.eslcafe.com

This "Internet Meeting Place" can be accessed by teachers and students alike. The easily navigated site offers resources such as idioms, pronunciation help, a photo gallery, and an "idea cookbook" for teachers.

Songs for Teaching: EFL/ESOL/ESL Songs and Activities

http://www.songsforteaching.com/esleflesol.htm

Lyrics and sound clips are offered for a variety of songs that help students learn vocabulary for things such as colors, shapes, and food, among many other topics.

Marie Nuzzi's List of Valuable ESL Resources

http://www.eslconnect.com/links.html

This gateway site offers links to scores of other useful ESL sites. The sites are helpfully organized by topics such as ESL Lessons, Homework Help, Crosswords and Puzzles, and English Teaching Ideas.

ESLgold.com

http://www.eslgold.com/site.jsp?resource=pag_ex_home

This website provides English teaching and learning materials at no cost for both students and teachers. Resources are organized by skill and level and by topic labels such as listening, speaking, writing, and vocabulary.

esl-lounge.com

http://www.esl-lounge.com

Teachers can download free lesson plans, learning activities, and worksheets for ESL classroom teaching at this site. Other resources include board games, flashcards, and song lyrics ready for use.

ESL Partyland

http://www.eslpartyland.com

Billed as "the cool way to learn English," this website allows users to enter depending on whether they are a teacher or a student. Students can access interactive quizzes, discussion forums, a chat room, and interactive lessons on a variety of topics. Teachers can download lesson plans and reproducible materials, contact other educators, and connect to other useful links.

Internet TESL Journal: Selected Links

http://iteslj.org/ESL.html

Maintained by a professional journal, this website compiles the best Internet sites for ESL and EFL students. Criteria used were ease of navigation, lack of advertising, and utility for students.

Pizzaz!

http://darkwing.uoregon.edu/~leslieob/pizzaz.html

Billed as the website for "People Interested in Zippy and ZAny Zcribbling," these writing activities are appropriate for beginner through advanced ESOL student levels.

The ESL Area: Tips for Teachers

http://members.aol.com/adrmoser/tips/tips.html

This helpful site maintained by teachers provides handouts, checklists, and articles that can be downloaded for free. Three features in particular should be noted: Communicating with

Students and Families, Teaching Content to ESL Students, and Teaching ESL Students to Use the Internet. Some of the information for parents is available in Spanish.

CULTURAL DIFFERENCES AMONG LEARNERS

Celebrating Diversity: Calendar

http://www3.kumc.edu/diversity

Maintained by the University of Kansas, this site offers month-by-month multicultural celebrations, many of them with links to other sites for background information or classroom activities. Users can also browse by religious holidays, ethnic holidays, and national holidays.

Center for Research on Education, Diversity & Excellence

http://www.crede.org

CREDE is a federally funded program that aims to improve the education of students from diverse backgrounds (including culture, language, ethnicity, geographic location, and poverty). The website includes teaching tools, effective demonstrations, a glossary, and links to hundreds of other sites.

Diversity Dictionary

http://www.inform.umd.edu/EdRes/Topic/Diversity/Reference/divdic.html

Words and terms related to diversity issues are defined on this website. Users can also find links to resources related to specific issues such as gender, ethnicity, religion, and national origin

The Human Diversity Resource Page

http://community-2.webtv.net/SoundBehavior/DIVERSITYFORSOUND

This gateway site is dedicated to promoting appreciation of human diversity. Links to multicultural posters, calendars, and cross-cultural resources—just to name a few—are provided.

Multicultural Pavilion

http://www.edchange.org/multicultural

Teachers can access a wealth of information and activities on Multicultural Pavilion. Most noteworthy are classroom-ready awareness activities, a multicultural awareness quiz, and a Teacher's Corner with free handouts and resource links.

Reprinted with permission.

Multicultural Song Index

http://www.edchange.org/multicultural/arts/songs.html

Popular music can be an effective way to initiate discussions about multicultural issues. This website compiles popular songs and organizes them by topic: race and ethnicity, social class, age, gender, and others.

National PTA: Respecting Differences

http://www.users.interport.net/m/e/melissad.enteract/cfplus/oc/ococt01/ensuring.asp

Links to a variety of articles and resources are available on topics such as multiethnic children and families, prejudice and hatred, and cross-cultural friendships. The *Checklist for Quality Indicators* is a helpful self-evaluation to help schools examine the current status of parent and family involvement. Appendix A in the PDF file is available in Cambodian, Chinese, English, Korean, Spanish, and Vietnamese.

GIFTED EDUCATION

National Association for Gifted Children

http://www.nagc.org

This national, nonprofit organization's website offers teachers information about resources to help gifted and talented children develop to their full potential. Be sure to visit the Parent Information page for an excellent discussion on the characteristic of gifted students.

Reprinted with permission.

Davidson Institute for Talent Development

http://www.ditd.org

The Getting Started area of this website has separate entry portals for parents, educators, and students. Teachers can review FAQs, access an online library, and browse resources by topic.

Fonetiks

http://fonetiks.org

This free, online pronunciation guide helps users with pronunciation in seven varieties of English. Pronunciation samples from native speakers are provided as well as common sentence patterns.

Gifted Development Center

http://www.gifteddevelopment.com/

Teachers can learn about the characteristics of gifted students, facts about IQ tests, and gain access to scores of other useful links.

Gifted Resource Center

http://www.educationaladvancement.org/resources/about_sdb.php

The Institute for Educational Advancement is dedicated to supporting educational practices that help gifted and talented students develop their full potential. Particularly helpful to teachers on this website are the Additional Resources section, the FAQs, and the Glossary.

Hoagies's Gifted Education Page

www.hoagiesgifted.org

This website offers resources and links for teachers, parents, and students. If entered through the Educators page, teachers will find discussions of acronyms and terms used in the field, essays and articles on pertinent topics, and ideas for curriculum modifications. The Kids page features reading lists, games, and more.

National Research Center on the Gifted and Talented

http://curry.edschool.virginia.edu/gifted/projects/NRC/

One of two research centers in the nation, this website provides a Resources page listing recommended books, articles, and websites. Hott Linx offers support for differentiated instruction.

SENG: Supporting Emotional Needs of the Gifted

http://www.sengiftcd.org

SENG's mission is to provide resources and information for developing supportive environments for gifted children. There is an Articles Library, a list of Recommended Reading, ideas for getting involved, and a special forum just for parents.

Uniquely Gifted

http://www.uniquelygifted.org

This website is dedicated to providing resources for those who work with gifted children who also have disabilities or special needs. Meeting the needs of twice-exceptional children is a relatively new educational topic. This website points users to useful books, discussion of popular treatments, appropriate assessments, and personal stories and case studies.

World Council for Gifted and Talented Children

http://www.worldgifted.ca

This international organization offers resources to educators around the globe. The World Resources page recommends excellent children's print materials, kids' resources, and links to other organizations.

INCLUSION AND MAINSTREAMING OF PEOPLE WITH DISABILITIES

Council for Exceptional Children

http://www.cec.sped.org/index.html

The CEC is the largest international professional organization dedicated to improving the education of students with exceptionalities. Resources, professional development opportunities, and information on effective classroom practices are available through the CEC website.

Focus on Learning

http://www.focusonlearning.org/learning.htm

This excellent website provides parents and teachers with support, learning resources, and legal information. The Tips for Parents section is equally useful for educators.

Kathy Schrock's Guide for Educators: Special Education

http://school.discovery.com/schrockguide/edspec.html

This award-winning Discovery School site serves as a gateway to other websites. Topics include American Sign Language, disability resources, gifted and talented education, and speech development.

LD OnLine

http://www.ldonline.org

This well-organized site features a state-by-state guide, directories, a bulletin board, and an Ask the Expert section. Separate entry portals for parents and kids are also available.

Learning Disabilities Resource Community

http://www.ldrc.ca/about.php

The Learning Disabilities Resource Community (LDRC) provides information and communication tools for educators who work with those with learning disabilities. This is a great background information site where teachers can access definitions, directories, and newsletters.

Songs for Teaching: Music for Children and Teens with Special Needs

http://www.songsforteaching.com/specialneeds.htm

Lyrics and sound clips are provided for songs that use music to promote learning and skills development. Teachers can select from categories such as physical challenges, speech development and articulation, and autism.

National Dissemination Center for Children with Disabilities

http://www.nichcy.org

This website serves as a central source of information on children's disabilities, special education legislation, and research-based information on effective educational practices.

Special Education Resources on the Internet

http://www.seriweb.com

SERI is a collection of Internet resources with links to a variety of special education topics such as learning disabilities, physical and health disorders, vision and hearing impairment, and legal resources.

Special Needs Opportunity Windows

http://snow.utoronto.ca/resources

SNOW helps users access Web resources related to special needs, adaptive technologies, and education. This site includes information on adaptive technologies, social and educational resources, specific disabilities such as autism, blindness, speech impairment, and more.

University of Virginia: Special Education

http://curry.edschool.virginia.edu/go/specialed

The Curry School at the University of Virginia maintains an excellent website on special education resources. Here educators can learn about the history of special education, specific disabilities, and links to other special education resources on the Internet. There is also a section for parents and students who need special education.

AT-RISK YOUTH AND CHILDREN IN CRISIS

The Department of Education estimates that approximately 11 to 48 percent of children in the United States can be considered "at risk." In addition to teaching the curriculum and managing a classroom, educators also have to contend with issues that are often outside their purview. The following websites will provide resources for working with troubled youth. However, take note that many Internet resources are listed under specific crises (e.g., dropout prevention, families in poverty, drug or alcohol use). So if you have a specific issue in your classroom, you should do a search on that particular topic on one of the main search engines.

National Dropout Prevention Center/Network

http://www.dropoutprevention.org

This support network for practitioners offers resources for increasing student retention. Links to hundreds of other sites (many for students and their families) underscore the strategies and interventions that have proved to be most effective.

Reprinted with permission.

Effective Schooling Practices and At-Risk Youth: What the Research Shows

http://www.nwrel.org/scpd/sirs/1/topsyn1.html

The Northwest Regional Educational Laboratory publishes a School Improvement Research Series. This essay from the series is an excellent, accessible discussion on the characteristics of at-risk youth and effective schools.

The Prevention Researcher

http://www.tpronline.org/resourcesection.cfm

The subject index on this page is broken down by topics such as substance use, bullying, depression, and pregnancy prevention. Users can also access information by ethnic orientation such as African-American youth, Latino/Hispanic youth, and Native American youth.

Search Institute: 40 Developmental Assets

http://www.search-institute.org/assets

The Search Institute is a nonprofit organization whose central mission is to "promote healthy children, youth, and communities." The Institute has developed 40 developmental "assets" that lead to caring and responsible adulthood.

U.S. Department of Education: School Dropout Prevention Program

http://www.ed.gov/programs/dropout/dropoutprogram.html

The U.S. Department of Education's website provides information and research on dropout prevention strategies.

FAMILY INVOLVEMENT IN EDUCATION

Both research and anecdotal evidence underscore that when parents are involved in their children's education, students do better in school. These websites will give you ideas for increasing parental participation in your classroom and school.

National PTA: Parent Resources

http://www.pta.org/parent_resources.html

The National PTA website provides parents with many helpful resources, including ideas for getting involved in children's schools, how to recognize a bully, and school dress codes.

Reprinted with permission from National PTA.

The Collaborative for Academic, Social, and Emotional Learning

http://www.casel.org/about_sel/SELhome.php

CASEL provides information packets for teachers and parents. Especially useful are the free handouts that can be downloaded in both English and Spanish.

Crede

http://www.crede.org/links/4families.html

CREDE (see the Cultural Differences among Learners section on page 111) offers dozens of links for families. The broad range of topics include testing, educational presses, and parent networks.

The Family Involvement Network of Educators

http://www.gse.harvard.edu/hfrp/projects/fine.html

This national network offers several outstanding resources for both educators and parents, including bibliographies, publications, and teaching cases.

National Coalition for Parent Involvement in Education

http://www.ncpie.org

Both parents and educators will find the Action Briefs helpful in understanding a wide range of issues. Ideas for developing partnerships are presented and resources are conveniently categorized by audience (e.g., parents, educators, and administrators), by subject, and by professional organization.

National Council for Community and Education Partnerships

http://www.edpartnerships.org

The NCCEP's mission is to "develop and strengthen broadbased partnerships throughout the education continuum." Particularly useful are the Effective Practices Toolkits and the Virtual Communities Web pages.

National Education Association: Help for Parents

http://www.nea.org/parents/index.html

This easily navigable site provides accessible resources for parents on topics such as standardized testing, research that links parental involvement and school success, making the most of teacher-parent conferences, and parental volunteering in schools.

PTOtoday

http://www.ptotoday.com

A tremendous resource for K–8 parent leaders, this website offers a magazine and links to many useful resources. PTOtoday.com has ideas for school family nights, fundraising, and arts and enrichment. The organization also hosts a yearly conference and facilitates a national network.

 CHECK THEM OUT!
The Companion Website at **www.prenhall.com/cruz** has **Bonus Links** that are not included in the textbook!

CHAPTER 13

Teachers' Tool Kit

> **☞ REMEMBER!**
> Visit the Companion Website at **www.prenhall.com/cruz** for links to each website in this book.

Like professional carpenters who have tool kits for specialized instruments to help them do their job, elementary school teachers similarly need to have a "tool kit" at the ready. This chapter includes websites that will help you find resources and answers to a variety of classroom issues and needs.

CLASSROOM MANAGEMENT

WonderWise Parent Resource

http://www.k-state.edu/wwparent/courses/index.htm

This site, although designed for parents, offers extraordinary insights into how to structure interpersonal communications with children using the responsive discipline model.

Discipline Help: You Can Handle Them All

http://www.disciplinehelp.com/

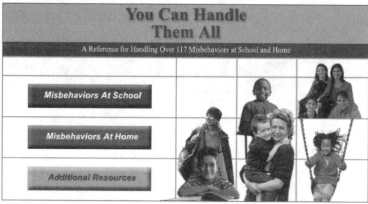

Reprinted with permission from the MASTER Teacher, Inc.

This site has extensive information on the reasons and sources for most classroom misbehavior. For 117 misbehaviors, Discipline Help identifies the primary causes, best strategies, and most common mistakes made in handling the misbehavior.

Education World

http://www.educationworld.com/a_curr/archives/shore.shtml

Under Classroom Problem Solver, the information on how to deal with commonplace problems is organized by topic such as The Chair Tipper, Bullying, and The Assembly.

TeacherVision: Behavior Management Forms

http://www.teachervision.fen.com/page/6283.html

TeacherVision provides various charts, forms, and contracts to monitor and track your students' behavior. Also at TeacherVision (http://www.teachervision.fen.com/page/6495.html) are tips from experienced teachers.

Dr. Mac's Amazing Behavior Management Advice Site

http://maxweber.hunter.cuny.edu/pub/eres/EDSPC715_MCINTYRE/715HomePage.html

This site offers thousands of tips on managing student behavior and provides step-by-step directions for implementing a great number of standard interventions. It also contains a bulletin board on which you can post your concerns and receive suggestions from teachers around the world.

Works4Me

http://www.nea.org/helpfrom/growing/works4me/library.html

This NEA site offers suggestions on preventive classroom management as well as how to handle problems when they do arise.

The Really Big List of Classroom Management Resources

http://drwilliampmartin.tripod.com/classm.html

Hundreds of clickable links to hundreds of resources on classroom management can be found at this site.

ONLINE PUBLICATIONS

The American Federation of Teachers

http://www.aft.org/teachers/index.htm

The AFT represents the economic, social, and professional interests of 1.3 million classroom teachers, and it publishes the highly respected *The American Educator*. At this site you can find AFT position papers and analysis of current topics affecting the education profession.

edweek.org

http://www.edweek.org/tm/index.html

This site includes discussion of contemporary educational issues, practical teaching advice and solutions, recommended books for teachers and students, summaries of research, and commentaries on a wide variety of topics from the magazines *Education Week* and *Teacher Magazine*.

The New York Times Learning Network

http://www.nytimes.com/learning

In addition to providing up-to-the-minute information on current events, the Learning Network links users to additional news and education resources on the World Wide Web. Its strength lies in the considerable archives of its host, *The New York Times*. Teachers will find the daily lesson plans—with thematic connections across the curriculum—very useful. Students will like the interactive news quizzes and the opportunity to send questions to *Times* reporters.

Teaching PreK-8 Magazine

http://www.teachingk-8.com

The popular magazine's website offers some free resources and additional resources for subscribers.

Time for Kids

http://www.timeforkids.com

At this online version of the print magazine, elementary students can select from the Grades 2–3 and Grades 4–7 renditions.

Reprinted with permission.

Weekly Reader

http://www.weeklyreader.com

This children's magazine offers games, activities, puzzles, and online reports that teachers can use in the classroom.

Children's Express

http://www.childrens-express.org

Although this is a British site, it includes topics of interest to all children worldwide, such as zero tolerance, classroom misbehavior, and so on, and each story is written by a youngster.

Scholastic

http://teacher.scholastic.com/index.htm

The online version of the popular school magazine offers a number of classroom-tested resources, ideas, and materials organized by grade level and topic.

Online NewsHour

http://www.pbs.org/newshour

The website of the popular television news show with Jim Lehrer offers transcripts of current broadcasts (some segments are available in RealAudio). Also included are background briefings, a discussion forum, and an archive, among other features.

NewsLink

http://newslink.org/

This site offers thousands of neatly organized links to newspapers, magazines, television and radio stations, and news services worldwide and is organized by states or top sites.

CNN.com

http://www.cnn.com

The cable network's home page includes up-to-the-minute news coverage on a variety of topics. Because it is based on the television show, nearly all of the stories are accompanied by an image or map. Users can also listen to stories in RealAudio, view video clips, and search the archives.

HANDOUTS, GRAPHIC ORGANIZERS, GAMES, AND PUZZLES

Region 15 Graphic Organizers

http://www.region15.org/curriculum/graphicorg.html

This regional school district in Connecticut has a well-organized listing of graphic organizers that come in both English and Spanish.

TeacherVision.com Graphic Organizers

http://www.teachervision.fen.com/page/6293.html?detoured=1&for_printing=1

This site offers almost 50 printable graphic organizers that are used primarily in the elementary school classroom.

KidsCom

http://www.kidscom.com/games/games.html

This is a game site for kids and the kind of resource that can be set up at a PC station for kids to use who finish projects early.

School Express

http://www.schoolexpress.com/fwsindex.php

This site has over 6,800 worksheets that are downloadable and categorized by teaching fields.

Puzzlemaker

http://www.puzzlemaker.com

Puzzlemaker is a puzzle generation tool for teachers, students, and parents. Create and print customized word search, crossword, and math puzzles using your word lists.

AIMS Education Foundation

http://www.aimsedu.org/Puzzle/index.html

Since 1995, this foundation has posted science/math puzzles that require kids to figure out solutions. A typical challenge is the classic puzzle requiring someone to move exactly three toothpicks in three triangles made up of three toothpicks each into an arrangement to make five triangles!

Education World's Brain Teasers

http://www.educationworld.com/a_lesson/lesson/lesson118.shtml

At Education World, their puzzles are called Brain Teasers.

Reprinted with permission from Educator World.

Jefferson Lab

http://education.jlab.org/indexpages/elementgames.html

The Jefferson Lab has science and mathematics games and puzzles.

ASSESSMENT AND RUBRICS

Kathy Schrock's Guides for Educators: Teacher Helpers

http://school.discovery.com/schrockguide/assess.html

This site offers an extensive listing of materials for assessment. These include articles on traditional and alternative assessment, teachers' comments for report cards, and rubrics that you can modify to meet your particular needs.

RubiStar

http://rubistar.4teachers.org/index.php

Teachers can easily build customizable rubrics for students for a wide variety of project types using this online interactive technology.

Rubrics at About Education

http://712educators.about.com/cs/rubrics/a/rubrics.htm

This site not only provides a number of detailed examples of rubrics in the different disciplines, but also explains why they are useful and effective.

The Chicago Public Schools Assessment Ideas and Rubrics

http://intranet.cps.k12.il.us/Assessments/Ideas_and_Rubrics/ideas_and_rubrics.html

This site includes a rubrics bank with a large number of samples for the various disciplines.

Project Based Learning

http://pblchecklist.4teachers.org/

PBL is an interactive site that walks you through a process to create checklists for writing, science, and public speaking tasks by grade level in both English and Spanish.

EDUCATION LAW

Education Law Association

http://www.educationlaw.org/links.htm

This page from the ELA's website offers a number of links to legal resources for educators. In addition to using search engines and directories, you can access online publications and federal resources.

Wrightslaw: Teachers, Principals, Paraprofessionals

http://www.wrightslaw.com/info/teach.index.htm

Originally developed with a focus on the rights of children with disabilities, this site offers information on a variety of legal education issues.

GENERAL RESOURCES

abcteach

http://abcteach.com/

This site has over 5,000 printables that include worksheets, word walls, assignment books, certificates, portfolio dividers, and number puzzles.

Reprinted with permission.

FreeImages.com

http://www.freeimages.com/photos/

At Free Images you can search or browse images by category that you can use in your classroom.

FamilyEducation

http://www.familyeducation.com/home

Broken down by grade levels (Pre-K–2, 3–5, 6–12), this site offers advice and resources on important topics such as school safety and standardized tests. Free printables are also available and accessible by grade level and subject matter.

PBS TeacherSource

http://www.pbs.org/teachersource

This high-quality site can be browsed by subject field, and PBS regularly features newly developed topical lesson plans.

Home2School

http://www.home2school.com

Intended primarily as a resource for parents to help their children with schoolwork, this interactive site offers refresher activities on a wide range of school subjects, suggests a children's reading list that can be searched by topic or grade level, and allows users to create a personalized education plan based on state standards.

TeacherVision.com

http://www.teachervision.fen.com

In addition to the excellent lesson plans, this site synthesizes current research on classroom management, provides an online grade book, and offers free, printable books for use in the classroom.

Work Essentials for Elementary School Teachers

http://office.microsoft.com/en-us/FX011433021033.aspx

This site has free downloads, templates for "good news reports" to the home, classroom newsletters, clipart, and so on.

NorthWest Regional Education Laboratory

http://www.nwrel.org/comm/hot.html

NWREL's goal is to improve educational results for children by providing research and development assistance in delivering equitable, high-quality educational programs by providing the results of research those teachers can use. At this site, you can see a list of topics.

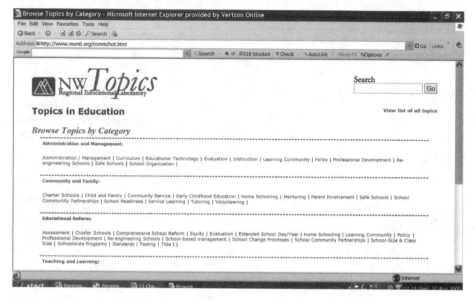

Reprinted with permission from Northwest Regional Educational Laboratory.

Glossary of Instructional Strategies

http://glossary.plasmalink.com/glossary.html

The glossary offers definitions of the frequently used terms to describe methods and approaches to teaching with hyperlinks to examples or essays.

HomeworkSpot

http://homeworkspot.com/

The HomeworkSpot is a multipurpose gateway to atlases, encyclopedias, dictionaries, current events, homework hotlines, and more.

CNET Download

http://www.download.com/

AT CNET, you can download freeware and shareware that can help you with your teaching and administrative duties.

CEO Express

http://www.ceoexpress.com/default.asp

CEO Express has one of the best catalogued and easily navigable gateways to resources for Internet users. As an example, go to Essential Downloads and click on Kids Software.

Federal Resources for Educational Excellence

http://www.ed.gov/free/index.html

This site provides a gateway not only to government resources, but also to various lesson plans by subject field.

 ✍ **CHECK THEM OUT!**

The Companion Website at **www.prenhall.com/cruz** has **Bonus Links** that are not included in the textbook!

CHAPTER 14

Students' Tool Kit

> **REMEMBER!**
> Visit the Companion Website at **www.prenhall.com/cruz** for links to each website in this book.

The World Wide Web provides a myriad of kid-friendly resources appropriate for student use both inside and outside the classroom. This chapter presents the best sites for students organized by these categories:

- Reference Resources
- Homework Help
- General Sites for Children

REFERENCE RESOURCES

Ask Jeeves Kids

http://www.ajkids.com

This kid-friendly search engine allows students to input their query in the form of a question. In addition to sections such as Fun & Games and News Resources, this site includes study tools such as Math Help, Almanac, and Clip Art.

Encyclopedia Britannica

http://www.britannica.com

In addition to the main search engine, which simultaneously searches the encyclopedia, the dictionary, and the thesaurus, this website offers interesting features such as Biography of the Day, This Day in History, Timelines, and a World Atlas.

Encyclopedia.com

http://www.encyclopedia.com

This is a useful, student-friendly encyclopedia site that also offers a dictionary, almanac, thesaurus, and links to other encyclopedias.

Fact Monster Dictionary

http://www.factmonster.com/dictionary.html

Students will appreciate not only the general dictionary search engine provided on this site, but also the special features such as Foreign Words and Phrases, Easily Confused Words, and Frequently Misspelled Words.

Federal Resources for Educational Excellence

http://www.ed.gov/free/kids.html

This government gateway site organizes student resources by subject area, such as language arts, mathematics, science, social studies, and foreign languages, and is best for the upper elementary grades. A short description of each link is provided to help students decide which are most appropriate for their usage.

Infoplease Atlas

http://www.factmonster.com/atlas/index.html

This online atlas includes printable maps, interactive maps, country and state profiles, and world and U.S. statistics. Students will enjoy testing their knowledge in the Crosswords and Quizzes sections.

Kidport Reference Library

http://www.kidport.com/RefLib/RefLib.htm

For students looking for reference resources as they work on a project, this online reference library offers links for science, social studies, language arts, creative arts, and general reference links.

KidsClick!

http://kidsclick.org

Created and maintained by librarians, this online research tool helps students find specific information quickly and easily. In addition to traditional academic subject areas, this site also has categories such as Weird & Mysterious, Computers & the Internet, and Home & Household.

Reprinted with permission.

Lexington Elementary School Libraries

http://lps.lexingtonma.org/Libdept/elem.html

This site includes Web pages for K–5 students with research links reviewed and selected by the librarians of the Lexington Public Schools, Lexington, MA.

HOMEWORK HELP

Fact Monster Homework Center

http://www.factmonster.com/homework/index.html

Organized by school subjects and academic skills (such as writing and studying), this website also provides handy tools such as a calculator, conversion charts, and periodic tables.

Scholastic Homework Hub

http://www.scholastic.com/kids/homework

This excellent site helps students research, guides their writing efforts, and offers tips for studying, testing, and getting organized.

Discovery School Homework Helper

http://school.discovery.com/homeworkhelp/bjpinchbeck/

Maintained by a student, this site contains over 700 links to sites that can assist students with homework. In addition to the traditional school subjects, links are also broken down by categories such as News, Reference, and Search Engines.

Study Hall

http://www.americatakingaction.com/studyhall/

This website provides online assistance for students who need help with schoolwork. In addition to having all the major content areas represented, it has a special area for Preschool activities, a Teacher's Lounge, and a Parent Resource Center.

GENERAL SITES FOR CHILDREN

Fun Brain

http://www.funbrain.com

This site has an entertaining collection of puzzles, games, quizzes, and the like that help to develop thinking skills.

Fact Monster

http://www.factmonster.com/

Fact Monster is an online almanac, encyclopedia, dictionary, and homework helper all rolled into one. This is an excellent gateway site for children.

Reprinted with permission.

Kidlink

http://www.kidlink.org/english/general/intro.html

This grassroots organization helps build life skills in children so that they can communicate with kids around the world and learn to live in a global society. Activities in over a dozen languages are included.

Kids' Place

http://www.eduplace.com/kids

Especially for K–8 students, this entertaining site allows kids to play games that sharpen skills in science, math, reading, social studies, and more. The Brain Power section offers brain teasers, word puzzles, and Web-based activities. Although it is sponsored by a major school publisher (Houghton Mifflin), it offers a balanced selection of games, practice activities, and test preparation tips.

Mystery Net's Kids Mysteries

http://kids.mysterynet.com

Students love applying their logic and reasoning skills to solve kid-centered mysteries. This site also offers scary stories, magic tricks, and a mystery book store.

Kids Mysteries
Mysteries to solve, scary
stories, and magic tricks

Reprinted with permission.

National Geographic for Kids

http://www.nationalgeographic.com/kids

Although the emphasis here may be on geography, this site also features a plethora of games, stories, activities, and experiments. The Cartoon Factory allows kids to create their own cartoons by adding dialogue to lively images provided.

PBS Kids

http://pbskids.org

Links to children's favorite PBS television shows are here as well as games, stories, music, and coloring pages.

Scholastic Kids

http://www.scholastic.com/kids/

Sponsored by the well-known publisher, this site features many of their most popular books. Students will enjoy the Games & Contests page where they get to test their knowledge and skills. The Preschool Playground is an easily navigable site even for very young children.

Yahooligans!

http://yahooligans.yahoo.com

Subtitled as "the Web Guide for Kids," this gateway site provides both academic information as well as features children will find entertaining. Students can play games, download screensavers, exchange e-cards, and learn new jokes.

 CHECK THEM OUT!

The Companion Website at **www.prenhall.com/cruz** has **Bonus Links** that are not included in the textbook!

About the Authors

Bárbara C. Cruz is a Professor of Education at the University of South Florida. Her research interests include global and multicultural perspectives in education, with an emphasis on ethnic minority students, innovative teacher preparation practices, active learning strategies, and textbook bias. In addition to writing academic publications, she is the author of several Hispanic biographies and young adult books on educational issues such as school dress codes, single-sex education, and school violence.

Jimmy Duplass is a Professor of Education at the University of South Florida. His research focus is on technology integration, philosophical foundations of social sciences education, methods of instruction, and competing conceptions of curriculum. He has authored academic articles on topics such as values education, curriculum design, instructional methods, technology integration, thinking skills, and administrative practices in higher education and has received over $1 million in technology grants. Professor Duplass has three other textbooks in print.

DEAR TEACHER:

This book is designed for pre-service and in-service teachers, curriculum specialists, and home schoolers.

Think of us as your personal shopper for resources you can use from the Internet in the elementary school classroom.

With that goal in mind, we ask a favor of you.

- If you have used a great website that is not included in this book or on the Companion Website, please share it with us so that we might include it in the next edition of this book.

- If you find one of our links has changed or is no longer working, please let us know.

Please let us know how we can improve our book by sending us an e-mail message at **bcjd@coedu.usf.edu**.

Sincerely,

Bárbara C. Cruz

Jimmy Duplass